THE
Diva
PRINCIPLE

michelle mckinney hammond

HARVEST HOUSE PUBLISHERS

EUGENE, OREGON

Cover by Koechel Peterson & Associates, Inc., Minneapolis, Minnesota

Cover photo: Tom Henry / Koechel Peterson & Associates, Inc.

Published in association with the literary agency of Alive Communications, Inc., 7680 Goddard Street, Ste #200, Colorado Springs, CO 80920.

THE DIVA PRINCIPLE
Copyright © 2004 by Michelle McKinney Hammond
Published by Harvest House Publishers
Eugene, Oregon 97402
www.harvesthousepublishers.com

Library of Congress Cataloging-in-Publication Data

McKinney Hammond, Michelle, 1957–
  The diva principle / Michelle McKinney Hammond.
    p. cm.
  ISBN 0-7369-1153-7 (pbk.)
  1. Christian women—Religious life. 2. Attitude (Psychology)—Religious aspects—Christianity. 3. Women in the Bible—Biography. 4. Success—Religious aspects—Christianity. 5. Conduct of life. I. Title.
  BV4527.M418 2004
  248.8'43—dc22
                                           2003020638

Printed in the United States of America.

04 05 06 07 08 09 10 11 12 /VP-KB/ 10 9 8 7 6 5 4 3 2 1

Contents

Divas

THE WORLD HAS CELEBRATED

(and some they should)

Harriet Tubman

Barbra Streisand

Lena Horne

Jacqueline Kennedy Onassis

Marion Wright Edelman

Margaret Thatcher

Judith Jamison

Shirley Chisholm

The Delaney Sisters

Florence Griffith Joyner

Patti Labelle

Ann Richards

Cicely Tyson

Meryl Streep

Carmen de Lavallade

Mary Kay

Angela Davis

Helen Gurley Brown

Lady Diana

Princess Grace Kelly

Loretta Young

Maria Shriver

Sophia Loren

Andrea Jung

Mae Jemison

Condoleeza Rice

Lauren Bacall

Tina Brown

Barbara Walters

Eartha Kitt

Carly Fiorini

Josephine Baker

Zsa Zsa Gabor

Diane Sawyer

Eleanor Roosevelt

Orit Gadiesh

Leontyne Price

Ruby Dee

Vashti MacKenzie

Diana Ross

Mary, Queen of Scots

Betty Shabazz

Nina Simone

Madeleine Albright

Flori Roberts

DENIECE GRAVES

Elizabeth Taylor

Donna Karan

Nancy Wilson

Naomi Sims

Cleopatra

Tina Turner

Jane Fonda

Maxine Waters

Diahann Carroll

Mahalia Jackson

Zora Brown

Barbara Jordan

Sarah Vaughan

Mother Teresa

Mrs. Winston Churchill

Maya Angelou

Bette Davis

Josephine Premice

Audrey Hepburn

Iman

Sojourner Truth

Althea Gibson

Zora Neale Hurston

Katherine Battle

Maria Callas

Catherine Zeta Jones

Queen Elizabeth

Cheryl Lee Ralph

Gloria Vanderbilt

Pamela Thomas-Graham

Norma Kamali

Anna Wintour

Susan Taylor

Vera Wang

Madame C.J. Walker

Beyoncé Knowles

Marian Anderson

(If I've left off anyone, charge it to my ignorance and not to my heart.)

Divas
I HAVE MET OR KNOWN PERSONALLY

The Women in My Family

My mother—Norma McKinney

My sisters—Nicole Neal, Yaaba Panford-Faquir, Jacqueline White

My grandmothers—Alexandra Petrona Branker, Louise Fairchilds and Sarah Appiesam Hammond

My aunts—Mildred Squires, Ernesta Branker Forde, Eglantine White, and Marion Arkaah

My Mentors

P.B. Wilson, Terri McFaddin, and Lois Blackwell

Mighty and Special Women of God

Kay Arthur	Carol Kent	Barbara Skinner
Elizabeth George	Lindsey O'Connor	Marilyn Davis
Stormie Omartian	Vanessa Long	Devi Titus
Janice Chaffee	Lois Evans	Marilyn Warren
Rev. Elaine Flake	Shirley Rose	Gigi Graham
Cynthia Hale	Tammy Maltby	Mildred Harris
Beverly LaHaye	Shirley Hawkins	Susan Wales
Florence Littauer	Audrey Ash	Edith Tripp
Shaneen Clarke	Nancy Leigh DeMoss	Thelma Wells

My Faithful Inner Circle

In alphabetical order because they are all important!

Brenda Blonski, Sheila Frazier, Lydia Garlington, Nancy Heche, Kristi Jordan, Charlotte Kroot, Peggy Matthews, Karen McDonald, Theresa Hayden Powell, Pamela Shine, Jan Shirtz, Yvonne Holdbrook-Smith, Michelle Taylor, Holly Virden, Cindy Wierzba.

Calling All Divas and Wannabes!

Well ladies, here we are! Welcome to the beginning of a whole new attitude. Diva-tude. You've heard it a million times—attitude is everything. And indeed it is. What you believe definitely affects what you do. What you do affects the response from others or results you receive. What you receive affects your attitude toward life, which then affects your next move, which further affects the outcome of your actions, which will then have a profound effect on your joy level, your success, your fulfillment, your everything... whew! See how easy it is for life to fall into either a cycle of defeat or victory?

We're about to change all of that and get you on the road to success in every area of your life—from finance to romance. How? By renewing your mind so your life can be transformed into one of endless possibilities.

Can *you* achieve this diva-tude? Absolutely, but a little elbow grease is required to accomplish the task. Some dismantling of old unvictorious ideas and concepts needs to take place along with a rebuilding of your inner woman. Be forewarned, old habits die hard. This will be a workout for some and a welcome change for others. We are going to take a serious look at not only our inner attitudes but also our outer habits. The things we don't do as well as the things that we *do* do well and adjust where necessary. Someone once said that insanity is doing the same thing over and over while expecting different results. What changes are you ready for in your life? Are you willing to do the work to have your dreams come true? Here is where the rubber meets the road. Where the girls are separated from true women. The average from the divinely set apart.

Because you picked up this book, I believe you are searching for more. With that in mind, know you have just chosen a tool that can change your destiny if you apply the principles you learn. In the pages that follow, we will take a look at several diva profiles and glean attributes from their lives that qualified them for diva-hood. Some of the people I chose just might surprise you, but stick with me and the path will become clearer as we travel together. Remember, there is no such thing as an overnight success. For those who are successful, it is because of their diligence to refine themselves and their gifts. They are always prepared for the moment when opportunity knocks. Oh yes, opportunity will indeed knock. But if it doesn't find a prepared vessel, it moves on in search of someone who is ready to welcome success, love, or whatever the heart desires.

On that note, I encourage you to delight in the process of your transformation, taking it one day at a time. Give yourself a pat on the back for achieving a goal and don't beat yourself up if you miss it—just promise yourself you'll do better next time. Greatness takes time to achieve and you are already on your way to becoming a totally divine woman. Are you ready? Well let's get started...

Webster's Dictionary

Di•va: \n.\ [It, lit., fem. of divus, divine]
1a: PRIMA DONNA

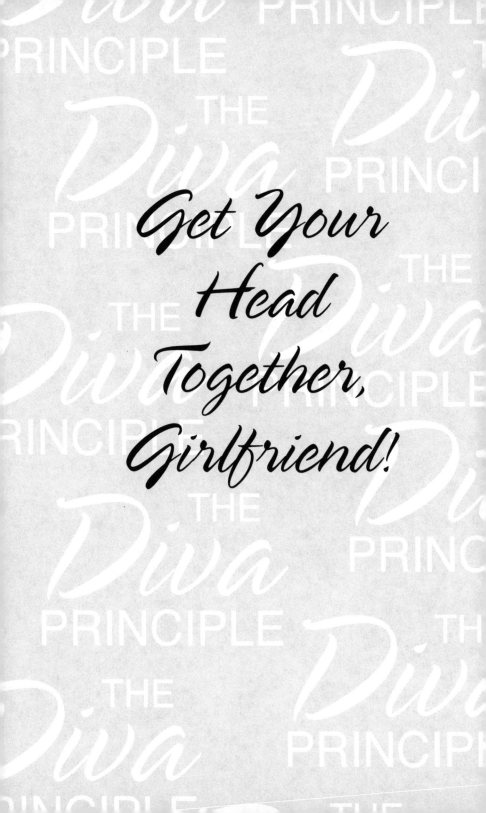

Get Your
Head
Together,
Girlfriend!

Diva Profile

The Shulammite Woman
(Song of Songs 1–8)

WHAT'S HER STORY:

She was a diva and didn't know it.

INSIDE SCOOP:

Some theologians say this young shepherdess came from Shunem, but the most popular rumor has it that she was actually Abishag, the young virgin who cared for and warmed the body of David, king of Israel, in his old age until he died. It was even speculated that she was married to David. This is why David's son Adonijah asked for her hand in marriage after David died; knowing that if he gained one of David's wives, he could also lay claim to his kingdom. Solomon, who had already been proclaimed king by David himself, saw through this traitorous plot and had Adonijah killed. It is also commonly thought that Solomon fell in love with her while she was in the palace, and when she was returned to her village after the death of King David, he pursued her and won her hand.

WEAKNESS:

Low self-esteem. Was a caregiver. Compared herself to others. Was overheard saying (in paraphrase), "Don't look down on me because of the darkness of my skin. I was ordered to take care of my brothers' vineyard and in the process of caring for their affairs, I have overlooked my own needs and not taken care of myself" (Song of Songs 1:6).

STRENGTH:

She did not compromise her morals and maintained her purity even though she was deeply in love.

DIVA-TUDE:

The realization that she is indeed loved, in spite of any real or imagined flaws, causes her to declare with confidence, "I am my beloved's and I know that I am the one that he desires" (Song of Songs 7:10).

THE TOUCH THAT MADE THE DIFFERENCE:

Her encounter with a king who loved her, wooed her, proclaimed her worth, and made her his own.

The Making of a Diva

*A*re divas born or made? That is the question. I believe divas are born. Building on that premise, I also believe there is a diva inside every woman. Deep down, underneath the layers of all the other things she has supposedly "learned" about herself—truth, fiction, deception, or just the superimposed bad feelings of others who do a real good job smothering the diva within—beats the heart of a diva just waiting to be released.

Weren't you surprised to find out the true definition of the word diva? I mean *really!* The word *prima donna* definitely has to be examined at its root. Prima donna actually means "first lady" and was used to describe the principal female singer in an opera or concert organization. This spoke of the level of her talent. She was primo, the best, unsurpassed by countless others, the crème de la crème! Later it evolved into being associated with an extremely vain, insensitive, or undisciplined person and that definition, for the most part, has stuck to present day. Perhaps the first opera divas began believing their own press and behaved badly, but for the purposes of this book we will investigate its original meaning of outstanding woman. The consummate woman. The *ultimate* woman. And in a man's mind...totally divine.

It has been said divas command attention without demanding it. There is just "something" about a true diva. There is an air of confidence, finesse, style, and originality mingled with a certain "je ne sais quoi" as the French would say in their grand manner. From the moment a diva steps into the room, everyone knows that "she" has arrived. Divas never just walk into a room, they arrive! Their bearing and manner sends the signal loud and clear that "I am a woman set apart." They never exit a room without leaving a part of themselves behind. A rich deposit of wisdom, an encouraging word, something seemingly intangible yet profound, that leaves a lasting impression on the hearts of those who interacted with them.

Indeed! Because we now know the first definition for diva is divine, we can totally attribute this special quality to being a God thing. A deposit of the divine nature of God was placed into the spirit of every woman when He breathed the breath of life into her and she became a living soul. In that moment, she was set apart for a unique purpose with divine credentials for living out her calling. A big, invisible stamp was placed on her that made everyone recognize she was special. But somewhere between infancy and womanhood, something happened—the diva within was lost. The small seed planted by the hand of God was crushed beneath disappointments, criticisms, negative experiences, bad choices, and unfruitful behavior she now regrets. Now is the time to shake the dust off and let that diva seed blossom and unfold!

What's so divine about being divine? Divinity and victory walk hand in hand. Second Peter 1:3 says, "His [God's] divine power has given us everything we need for life and godliness through our knowledge of him who called us by his own glory and goodness. Through these he has given us very great and precious promises so that through them you may participate in his divine nature and escape the corruption in the world caused by evil desires." To have the mind of Christ is a major prerequisite to living a life well lived, filled with purposeful decisions and security. If an all-knowing, all-powerful God is willing to share everything He knows with me, I'm all for it, aren't you? When we decide to embrace the fullness of our relationship with God, take and use His advice in every area of our life, we come out ahead of the game, smelling like a rose. Looking like a divine diva.

In order to become this total outstanding and victorious package, we need to make sure that everything in our lives is in divine order—spiritually, emotionally, and physically. Here's the key: Attitude is everything.

But how do you get the right diva-tude? How do you find the real you, the one that is worthy of celebrating, especially if your attitude has been formed by the opinions, affirmations, or criticisms of others? As my mother would say, opinions are like tushes—everyone has one. Someone else once said there are three views of who we are—ours, others, and God's. So who do we listen to? Ourselves? Others? God? You guessed it sister, God! His is the only valid opinion. He knows everything, sees everything, and understands every little thing about you. He's straightforward, honest, and ever optimistic about your divine possibilities. Others can only see you through their own experiences. Your personal view is also limited by your emotions and your baggage. However, when we are in relationship with our heavenly Father, we begin to see things through His eyes and the possibilities are not only divine...they are endless.

A diva is spiritual. She knows who she is and *whose* she is. She has embraced her Savior and yielded to the lordship of Jesus Christ. Under His instruction, she is empowered to see her circumstances clearly, make choices wisely, and reap a victorious life in the process. The spiritual diva does not compromise her standards and is unapologetically sold out to her Lord. The grass does not look greener on the other side because she is walking in the right pasture. Feeding off the fruit of the land and enjoying the scenery.

Maybe you are having a bit of a struggle. Perhaps you are like Miss Shulammite, our first diva profile. You might be in great shape but are distracted from all you could celebrate about yourself because of, like her, the condition of your skin. Perhaps it's deeper. Perhaps you can't see your own beauty because of the pain that masks it. Hurtful situations and memories that hide the real you from view. Perhaps no one has ever told you that you are beautiful, precious, gifted, amazing...divine.

The thing that we must take note of in the life of our very first diva is to go with the premise that if she did indeed care for King David in his last days, she learned something of her value while in the presence of a king. She was considered a life force for him. However, after returning home, out of the king's presence, back to those who "knew her when," she was taken down a few notches. You know the story. *Mmm...hmm,* whenever you get a little sadiddy around those who really know you, won't they put you right back in your place? "Girl, puh-leeeze!," they say. "And who do you think you are? Remember I knew you *when! Before* you became all of that!"

It's enough to deflate the toughest ego, which is why true spiritual divas leave their egos at the door and reach for higher understanding—not their own self-involved opinions. You will never be able to see yourself clearly through your own eyes—your "knows" is in the way. Get it? The things you think you already *know* about yourself stop you from getting a new perspective on your situation.

Spiritual divas are not moved by the opinion of others. They realize others can never know enough about them inside and out to render sound judgment that holds true for a lifetime. The most liberating truth you can ever accept is this—it is impossible to control the opinions of others. The only person you can control is yourself. The only way to overcome "stinkin' thinkin'" about yourself is to find out what God thinks about you.

Miss Shulammite had some serious self-esteem issues when she wasn't in the presence of the king. When she tried to go it alone, all she got was abused and wounded. Ah ha! But the minute her beloved showed up to praise her beauty, list her virtues, and expound on her value, not only did her view of herself change, others saw her in a different light as well.

Interesting what a man can do for a woman's psyche. But not just any man. A true spiritual diva does not allow her moods and emotions to be tossed to and fro just because of the presence and/or behavior of a man. She is rooted and grounded on a foundation that is infinitely deeper. She has a divine relationship with a *supernatural* man. Through her interaction with the Lover of her soul, she comes to know and understand that she is a well-kept, divinely loved woman who declares like the Shulammite did, "My beloved is mine, and I am his" (Song of Songs 2:16).

Something about knowing that you are loved and treasured translates into confidence and success. It's a beauty that goes beyond skin deep because everything that enhances it comes from within.

Don't fool yourself. No matter how lovely the external, if your spirit, heart, and mind are not in divine order you're just another pretty face. Now take a woman who wouldn't necessarily make you look twice on a slow day, add the light of love to her eyes and the spirit of God beating in her heart, and all of a sudden her countenance radiates something that draws us to her. It's almost magical, but actually it's not. It's downright divine.

So what's a diva to do? Throw out all the baggage and sweep out all the lies that make you the victim instead of the victor. If a simple shepherdess could become a queen, you can truly rise to diva stature. It's time to rearrange your mind, and to be quite honest, perhaps a few friendships and associations. Mike Murdoch, famed author and teacher, says it best, "Go where you are celebrated, not tolerated."

Diva Principles

Now let's take a look at some of the other components that gave our first diva her victorious attitude so we can apply them to our own lives.

Miss Shulammite knew the importance of having a relationship with the king. To think that he would love little ole her! She was just a shepherdess with no great royal background—a mere commoner, yet he saw her as a queen!

Well, my sister, God looks at you in the same light. There is nothing common about you to Him. He views you as His own divine handiwork and proclaims that you are a "good thing." Carefully molded and shaped just as you are. It is an insult to our Divine Creator when we fail to see the beauty of what He fashioned when He made us. Would you walk up to a painting and criticize it loudly while the artist was standing there? Well, that's what we do when we stand in front of the mirror and berate ourselves for all of our perceived flaws. The artist, God Himself, is present, and He is disappointed that you are not taking delight in His creation.

Why is it so important to embrace your own special brand of beauty and not compare yourself to others? Because the world's opinion changes with the wind. Thin is in, thin is out. Breasts are out, butts are in. I have to confess I've had a prominent tush all of my life that I've tried to minimize. It took one woman to come on the music scene and not apologize for her voluptuous assets to set us all free. And therein lies the secret. Perhaps if we celebrate what we have, others will join us. If we constantly apologize for our features, or say negative things about ourselves, others will help us with that, too.

Diva Confession

I will celebrate myself and acknowledge that I am a specially handcrafted addition to God's awesome creation.

The second big step in building self-confidence is sur-rounding yourself with the right support system. Miss Shu-lammite had a group of protective brothers and supportive sisters who challenged her when necessary, but were also there for her when she needed them. They acknowledged her beauty and virtue and applauded it. They also held her accountable to right living. Everyone needs a support system, not a wrecking crew. Surround yourself with those who see and nurture your gifts and exhort you to be better than you already are. Take stock in friends who will speak the truth to you in love, but extend grace to you as well. Ask God to send you a mentor to teach you how to master the art of womanhood. Every true diva had a grand diva she learned from. Select a woman who is living the life you want to live—successful, whole, and joyous. Ask her if she will walk with you and speak into your life. Learn from her vic-tories but also be willing to learn from your own mistakes.

Diva Confession

*I will disassociate from those who feed
me negativity. I will only surround
myself with those who provoke
and promote me to be the best I can be.*

Thirdly, know the value of your heart, your mind, and your body. Miss Shulammite was self-confident because she had not allowed herself to be used and discarded, emotion-ally bruised, or mishandled. She lived in a very protective environment but also kept herself pure. When her brothers asked her if she had been a door allowing men to enter or a wall keeping her virginity for the day of her marriage, she proudly proclaimed that she was a wall, her breasts were like towers, and she had found favor in the sight of the man who claimed her…(Song of Songs 8:10). She could stand tall in confidence and not be bowed over in shame under the weight of past issues…baggage. She found favor because her man could trust her in light of her character.

How many of us bear the scars of past relational mistakes that cause us to lose confidence when presented with a chance for love? Or worse yet, our mistakes have paralyzed us and caused us to repel love rather than attract it? Don't despair if you are not a physical virgin. Because of your relationship with the King, you've been given the chance to have a new beginning right now! Reclaim your virtue by developing a new attitude about your body and by setting boundaries to protect what should only be yours until a man commits his life to you at the altar—and not a day before.

Divas are chaste, understanding the worth and the value of their hearts and bodies and treating them as precious commodities. Not just anyone gains access to sample or touch, only one who is worthy. Your heart and your body must be earned by one who knows the true cost of love. A lifetime commitment in the form of marriage. To give your heart and your body before that time is to relinquish your power. When you are powerless, you are open to be deceived, used, taken advantage of, and disappointed. A virtuous diva knows that to be a secret garden enclosed—enveloped in mystery—is truly irresistible to the right suitor. She is willing to wait for the appropriate time to awaken love.

Diva Confession

*I will value myself, my heart, my mind,
and my body. I will not discount my love
or give away my pearls to those who are
not discerning of their worth.*

Last but not least, Miss Shulammite had something to offer besides herself. She had a vineyard to give to her king. Financial security is a big confidence booster, but it extends beyond that. What else do you have to offer besides physical beauty? Intelligence? Resourcefulness? The gift of hospitality? Creativity? Style? All things that we will cover later. A true diva, in order to be considered divine, needs to be a complete package. She must come bringing more than herself or what she wants to the party. Now is the time to complete the picture of who you are as a woman.

Diva Confession

*I will seek to be a complete gift to
those I love. I will not depend on merely the
external. I will cultivate and present
a bountiful offering of internal gifts
that nurture others.*

Diva Do's and Don'ts

🍥 Discard the negative, absorb the positive.

🍥 Do not volunteer to be a victim.

🍥 Examine your friends and associates closely. Who is bringing you down? How much of their negativity are you absorbing? About yourself? About life in general? Though I don't recommend ever cutting off associations, I do recommend reassigning positions in your life. Perhaps some should not be as close to you as they presently are and should be placed on another level of friendship. In some instances, you will need to part company if their input is constantly destructive.

🍥 Find out what God has to say about who you are. Discover your true value through His Word as well as by listing your attributes that bless others.

🍥 Decide to protect what is precious to you. Your heart, your body, your love. If trust and respect must be earned, so must your love.

🍥 Cultivate your character and your gifts. Do a self-examination of all your qualities and assets. Write them down. Divide them in two categories. Strengths and weaknesses. Prioritize what you need to work on in order of importance. Write down your goals and make a plan for how to fulfill them. Seek counsel if you must.

🍥 Take one day at a time. Begin to see the big picture of your life and purpose to work on all facets of being a divine woman—victorious and whole.

Div-otion

I praise you because I am fearfully and wonderfully made; your works are wonderful, I know that full well (Psalm 139:14).

O heavenly King, because I know You do all things well and I was fashioned by Your loving hands, I affirm today that I am a divine vessel of Your handiwork because of Your presence in my life. Amen.

Diva Profile

The Queen of Sheba
(1 Kings 10:1-13; 2 Chronicles 9:1-12)

WHAT'S HER STORY:

She knew the value of wisdom. She pursued and embraced it.

INSIDE SCOOP:

Wealthy and powerful in her own right, this Queen of the South (as she has been called) went on a pilgrimage to meet King Solomon of Israel. Having heard astonishing reports about his wisdom, she went to see for herself. The story goes, that upon her arrival, she tested him with hard questions and spoke to him about all that was in her heart. Solomon answered every one of her questions, never being at a loss for the right explanation. And when they were through, he gave her the grand tour of his domain. Upon seeing his wealth and the splendor of his surroundings, she was rendered speechless and could only declare, "Truly the half had not been told about your wisdom and your prosperity" (1 Kings 10:7). She then bestowed upon him 120 talents of gold, which amounted to about 3.5 million dollars, precious stones, and an abundance of rare spices that had never been seen before. Solomon, in turn, gave her everything her heart desired and sent her away with a rich bounty of gifts. It has been speculated that she took all he taught her about God back to her country and influenced her subjects. There is mention of her from an Ethiopian eunuch who later has an encounter with the disciple Philip in the book of Acts. Jesus also referred to the Queen of Sheba in Luke 11:31 saying one like her would put the current generation to shame because she embraced the wisdom of God.

POTENTIAL WEAKNESS:

Because of her powerful position and affluence, she could have been a proud woman who was not open to receiving instruction and certainly not open to displaying any signs of vulnerability. However, this was not the case.

STRENGTH:

The queen was willing to acknowledge what she did not know and openly seek the answers. She was able to give credit where credit was due and celebrate the strength of the man who stood before her. She was not given to jealousy or covetousness but was able to see the hand of God in all that Solomon was blessed with. She did not go seeking with her hands empty. She went bearing gifts and gave them extravagantly.

DIVA-TUDE:

The realization that the favor of God rested on Solomon's life and was the source of all his power, wisdom, and splendor made her declare, "Blessed be the LORD your God who delighted in you, setting you on his throne to be king for the Lord your God. Because your God has loved Israel, to establish them forever, therefore he made you king over them to do justice and righteousness" (2 Chronicles 9:8).

THE TOUCH THAT MADE THE DIFFERENCE:

Her encounter with a king who knew God and was submitted to His leading gave her a new perspective on her position in life as well as a deeper spiritual understanding.

The Foundation for Diva-hood

What are divas made of? Pure substance that begins with a healthy dose of wisdom—*that's* what divas are made of. There is no sadder scene than a beautiful woman entering a room, opening her mouth, and completely destroying her beauty with the things that proceed from her lips. Everyone has had a good laugh at dumb blonde jokes, but actually they are not funny. How sad that foolishness and folly can have such a disfiguring effect on a beautiful face. Or worse yet, foolishness can sway a beautiful woman to make such poor choices that her face and countenance are permanently scarred by disappointment, pain, and frustration. You can have style, but if you don't have good sense something is seriously wrong with the entire picture.

Wisdom is not just an accumulation of the right information, it is also the ability to apply it to one's life. Perhaps this is why we are encouraged in Scripture to make sure we get an understanding. Understanding cements your commitment to make wise choices and stick with doing the right thing even when you don't feel like it. Yes, even when you don't feel like it. Remember, medicine never tastes good going down, but you're a whole lot better for taking it.

How do we move from making foolish choices to wise ones? By recognizing the difference between folly and wisdom. One of my favorite books of the Bible is Proverbs. It contains universal truth—wisdom that will stick to the wall of your soul and prove its merit if you adhere to it. In Proverbs, Solomon describes wisdom and folly. Interestingly enough at first glance they don't seem to be that different from one another. They both stand in plain view. They both beckon those who lack understanding to join them for a feast they have prepared. Ah, but this is where the similarities end. Wisdom has built her house and has it firmly set on a foundation of seven strong pillars. She lives on the principles of prudence, knowledge, discretion, counsel, sound judgment, understanding, and power. She has things to say that are worthy of being heeded because she only speaks the truth. Her words are just, not crooked or perverse. Her instruction is always right and faultless. Therefore, when you embrace what she says, it will lead you to riches, honor, enduring wealth, and prosperity. Read it for yourself in Proverbs 8 and 9.

That's the upshot on wisdom. So what's the lowdown on Miss Folly? Notice both are female. One is a divine diva, the other is a perpetrator. Miss Folly has a raggedy house. You know how I know? Because Proverbs 14:1 tells us that the foolish woman tears down her house with her own hands. Now that translates down to a more practical level. In short, the foolish woman is known for living in perpetual drama— her personal life and all of her affairs are in constant disarray because of the foolish choices she makes. She is always the victim. You see, while Miss Folly invites you to her party, her initial invitation does not reveal that she is loud, undisciplined, and without knowledge. This is why she makes the same mistakes over and over again—because she lacks understanding. She believes in catching where catch can and worrying about the consequences later. Her philosophy is, "Stolen waters are sweet and food eaten in secret is delicious!" Never mind that it gives you heartburn. That you end up sick at heart after finding yourself caught in the clutches of your own error. Following her suggestions only propels you down the slippery path that leads to death—death of your joy, peace, important relationships, hopes, and even your self-esteem. Then she's off...leaving you in the wake of your mistakes to find and invite yet another victim to partake of her foolishness.

Ah, but wisdom serves rare delicacies and forget water! She serves *wine*. Her meal leaves you full and satisfied—intoxicated with joy and peace. Doesn't that sound lovely? Then choose the instruction of wisdom instead of silver, knowledge over choice gold, because wisdom is more precious than rubies. Nothing you desire can compare with her. Whether it be a man or material possessions, believe me, you will need wisdom to get them and *keep* them. Every true diva understands the need for acquiring and walking in wisdom.

The Queen of Sheba, in spite of all that she had already acquired and attained, was driven for more...not for more *things*, but for more wisdom. She heard that Solomon was a man who knew God and understood His ways so she decided to seek him out. She got more than she bargained for. She found a man who was astute, keen, and downright brilliant in all affairs. From how to run his kingdom, to how to manage people, to how to settle disputes, to how to acquire massive wealth, he balanced all these things well. She met a man who was not arrogant and stuck on himself, but one who was able to listen to her heart and answer its cry. A man who was sensitive as well as generous. Believe me, she had encountered many a man but something was different about this one. She attributed the difference to his relationship with God and it changed something within her. She returned to her country a different woman...wiser for the understanding of what she had found.

What can we learn from this woman? Several things stand out that I think we must note and apply to our own lives.

Diva Principles

First of all, in spite of all that she had accomplished and acquired, she realized there was something lacking in her life. She purposed to diligently pursue the missing ingredient—wisdom. Her determination to settle the quest of her heart overrode pride and any other façade that would have been tempting to maintain for a woman in her position. Though she was a powerful queen in her own right, she submitted herself to the king in humility. Transparent through and through, she exposed every area of her heart to him. She did not fear vulnerability because her hunger to have understanding was so great.

Today, many women struggle to master the delicate dance between strength and vulnerability. How do we maintain our femininity and softness in a world that has pushed us to the wall and forced many to fight our own battles?

More women are remaining single now than at any other time in history. Acquiring fast-paced jobs and high-profile positions. Building their own portfolios, buying their own property, and collecting their own baubles. They are becoming masters of their universes and, in a lot of ways, are leaving men in the dust! Men can be intimidated by our strength, yet they long to still be kings. And yet no man or woman is an island. Giving and taking, sharing life experiences and lessons learned, is invaluable.

God never intended for us to learn only from experience. It was His design that we also learn from His instruction. I always urge others to seek out someone who is successful and ask that person to share their wisdom. Don't just listen to them, really hear them and put their instruction into practice. Don't be too proud to admit your mistakes. If you want something different to happen, you must do something different. What sound piece of advice have you been overlooking because the pain of admitting that you were wrong seems greater than the pain of change? A diva is humble. She is honest—with herself and with others—and accepts truth and correction gracefully, knowing it is the key to her living a victorious life.

Diva Confession

I will be diligent in my pursuit of wisdom and remain transparent in the face of truth, honestly assessing my choices and actions and making changes where necessary. I will not be too proud to receive sound counsel.

The next diva principle we must examine about our fabulous queen is she didn't go looking for a handout. No, she went to Solomon with full hands! She had something to bring to the party—something to offer a king. She had her own rich resources. She did not lord these over him or present herself in a, "You should be impressed with me" attitude. She was not distracted by herself. She was on a mission in pursuit of truth and understanding, and she gave of what she had. Gold, something of lasting value; precious stones, something of beauty; and rare spices, something that was uniquely her and set her apart in his mind.

Whether dealing with a man, a mentor, someone in a position to further your standing in life, or a friend, it should never just be about what they can give to you. You must always be mindful of what you can give to them. You must be willing to exchange resources. Though Solomon was a man who had everything, she managed to find something he did not have, that would appeal to his senses (like spices), and offered it to him in bountiful measures. She also found something that was common ground, that spoke his language (Yes, that would be the gold. Even back then money talked.) and gave enough to make a statement. All of her gifts symbolized things of lasting value. Her statement was, "I'm not here to use you. I want to partner with you and share your wisdom." No one wants to feel taken advantage of. In all our interactions, we must be ever mindful of our secret agendas.

When friendships are not formed from the heart, they will die the moment one of the party's agendas has been fulfilled. In these cases, one always walks away feeling used, vowing never to be so free about sharing their resources again. But if a rich deposit is left in the other person's life, both are richer for the exchange. What spice do you have to add to someone else's life? What thing of beauty? What common ground or experience? How much are you willing to give while pursuing what you want? Divas are always considerate, never purposing to take more than they give.

Diva Confession

I will strive to be a gift to others, always seeking to enrich their lives as they enrich mine. I will not be afraid of my vulnerability, but rather will see it as a powerful tool for gaining favor, as well as my heart's desires.

Let's see... oh, this one is big! She gave praise where it was due. When gazing at the opulence of all that belonged to Solomon, girlfriend did not get jealous and was open with her admiration. She was actually happy for him, for all he had acquired and accomplished. Her attitude led Solomon to believe she did not have a covetous bone in her body. This keen insight made him want to give her anything she asked for. When generous spirits meet, they often give freely to one another. But when jealousy, envy, and strife enter the picture, everyone runs for cover, determining to protect what belongs to them. She was able to celebrate his good fortune without a twinge. This one is difficult.

Even among Christians, I have heard some wondering why God would bless another and not bless them in the same way. The answer to that is: God carefully considers what each of us can handle and blesses us accordingly. Some of the things we crave would actually be detrimental to our well-being in the long run. We must be able to trust God's choices for our lives. Perhaps our extraordinary queen did not get an attitude over all of Solomon's blessings because she understood where they came from. She recognized the hand of God in his life and even cited the reason why. Because of his great wisdom, sensitivity, and generosity, she could see why God had chosen him to be king over Israel. Never once did she think, "Oh, he thinks he's all *that!* I need to cut this brother down to size by not letting on that I am impressed." No sir! She freely gave praise and reaped the benefits of it all. From God to man, everyone responds to praise. A true diva is not stingy with her praise because she knows it costs her nothing and it enriches the lives of those around her.

Diva Confession

*I will recognize the source of all blessings
and allow God to bless whom He chooses.
In turn, I will celebrate the blessings
of others and allow them to increase
my faith, believing I, too, can receive
the desires of my heart.*

Diva Do's and Don'ts

- Choose wisdom and discipline yourself to reject foolishness no matter how tempting.

- Pursue knowledge spiritually and intellectually. Have an understanding of God, His word, and His ways. Have at least a general working knowledge of the world at-large. It facilitates intelligent conversation with interesting people you meet.

- Step out of your comfort zone and learn about someone or something that is foreign to you.

- Never be too proud to accept counsel from others who have proven to be wise.

- Realize that sense is not common. Educate yourself in order to have good sense in managing practical matters.

- Learn the value of discretion. Good judgment and sensitivity to others are rare, but highly esteemed traits.

- Never lord your position or accomplishments over anyone.

- Always celebrate the good fortune of others.

- Purpose to give praise and encouragement freely to others.

- Never approach anyone empty handed—be a gift even when you are seeking one.

Div-otion

Wisdom is supreme; therefore get wisdom. Though it cost all you have, get understanding (Proverbs 4:7).

Dear heavenly King, as the source of all divine wisdom, I ask that You will give me wisdom and instill the desire in me to follow Your instruction and walk in the way of understanding. Amen.

Diva Profile

Deborah, Judge of Israel
(Judges 4:4–5:31)

WHAT'S HER STORY:

She knew she was only as great as those who surrounded her. She empowered and led her subjects willingly.

INSIDE SCOOP:

Deborah was a wife, prophetess, and judge over Israel at a time when the country was being oppressed by the Canaanites. Obviously well-loved, she was called "a mother in Israel." As a prophetess, she was able to perceive the purposes of God and declare them to others. She used this gift to lead her people to victory. By encouraging Barak, the commander-in-chief, to go to war against the enemies of Israel, she shook the yoke of fear off of the people and they were able to advance the country toward victory.

POTENTIAL WEAKNESS:

Because of her position and ability to influence others, she could have sought glory for herself or made demands of the people to further her own agenda. Instead, she sought the heart of God and encouraged her charges to do His will. In the end, everyone played a part in the victory.

STRENGTH:

Her ability to inspire others to fulfill the call of God on their lives and encourage them to press past their apprehensions. She was able to graciously give credit where it was due and celebrate the victory of others without lifting herself up.

DIVA-TUDE:

After the victory was won, Deborah stayed focused on what made the victory possible by singing out to the people, "When leaders lead in Israel, When the people willingly offer themselves, Bless the LORD!…My heart is with the rulers of Israel Who offered themselves willingly with the people. Bless the LORD!" (Judges 5:2,9 NKJV).

THE TOUCH THAT MADE THE DIFFERENCE:

Her close relationship with God and the ability to hear His voice, coupled with her submission to His direction, made her an effective leader of the people and one who was able to remain humble. Her burden for the freedom of her people overrode any desire for personal glory.

The Driving Force Behind a Diva

We have all asked the question: Who am I and why am I here? Every one of us longs to know that our life has a greater meaning than what we see or experience in the day to day. You know the adage, "Who will cry for me when I die?" I recall attending the funeral of a woman many years ago where one after another rose to give accolade after accolade for the effect this woman had had on their lives. Her kindness and encouragement had birthed greatness in the hearts of many. I walked away that day with a deep longing to make a difference in the lives of others.

We all have our own agendas for why we long to make a statement in this world and leave our mark on the hearts of people. For some, it's a power trip. For others, it's personal validation. For a minority, it is the fulfillment of knowing God is pleased with their lives. Which category do you fall into?

Are you a prima donna? Singing, "It's all about me, me, me"? Or are you driven by the needs of others around you? That is the big question. A divine diva is not self-centered. She is all about building up and equipping others to be the best they can be. She is able to locate the gifts of others, nurture them, and make them grow. She is a "life-giver" as my friend Tammy Maltby would say. Blessings abound when we are productive and fruitful in our lives. Not only does our fruitfulness feed us, it feeds others.

The "crab in a bucket" syndrome is not a part of her mentality because she is already secure in her own worth. She is able to allow others around her to thrive in their callings and encourages them to do so without being threatened. She assists them in accomplishing their mission whenever possible. A diva is determined to see her counterparts rise to a level equal to or even greater than herself. She is fulfilled when she sees others living up to their fullest potential and enables them to enjoy the rewards of their labor without being beholden to her.

Deborah was such a woman, a true mother in spirit. It is interesting to note that her story speaks of her having a husband but does not mention if she had children. Her husband's name means "torches" or "lightning flashes." Could it be that though he was a man behind the scenes, he actually was a light on the path for her? Perhaps it was because of his support that she was able to be so gracious in her leadership to the tribes of Israel. In any case, she had a mothering spirit those around her responded to. As a prophetess, she heard from God about the affairs of her people as well as the country. She administered justice, settled disputes, and righted wrongs. She literally presided over the nation under the direction of God.

It is with this insight we consider her posture. The story goes she *sat* under a palm tree and the children of Israel came to her for her to judge them…Read and learn. So many women are quick to offer advice and suggestions when they have not been asked for. I have found advice is better received when it has been sought. That is the first clue that the person is ready to hear something other than what they have already considered. Miss Deborah *sat*. And the people came to her.

She rested in her position, never insisting on pushing her weight around or being heard. She possessed the attitude, "let those who seek wisdom come." Being sensitive in the spirit, she also knew when to reach out. Not when she thought she should, but when prompted by the spirit of God. And even this was done with open hands. She sent for Barak, the leader of the army, and encouraged him to be obedient to the Lord. To go into battle and rest assured he would win. Barak refused to go without her so she agreed to go with him.

Now this deserves a sidebar. Ladies, know and recognize that sometimes the man in your life needs your encouragement, assistance, and inspirational presence in order to win the battles in his life. Deborah did not berate Barak and ask him, "What's wrong with you? Can't you do that by yourself? You are a *man* aren't you? Do I have to do *everything?*" This would be very undiva-like conversation. She agreed to go but also let him know his refusal to go alone would water down his claim on the victory. "There will be no glory for you in the journey you are taking," she said. "For the Lord will sell Sisera [the captain of the enemy army] into the hand of a woman" (Judges 4:9 NKJV). That was fine with him, so off they went together. The willing leader and the willing follower.

It is a difficult time for men today surrounded by so many strong women in the world. Perhaps it wasn't that much different back then, though I do believe for different reasons. In some instances, God will use women to accomplish things when men abdicate their posts. But whether in a place of being protected or out on the battlefront, women must know of their unique position and importance in a man's life. Sometimes a woman forgets what she represents in the life of a man. To Barak, I think Deborah's presence was a confirmation that God was indeed going with him into the battle. A man needs a woman to have his back because of what it signifies to him. He counts on her presence, as well as her prayers, to give him the strength to fight his way through the rough places in life. Some men can admit this, some men can't. True divas know for a fact the power they have in the life of a man and how to use it effectively.

On a more general note, Deborah did not treat Barak as an underling even though he was not on her level. She could have berated him and told him she was not going with him because the battle was not her job...you get the picture. No, instead she partnered with him, treating him as an equal, walking alongside him in his endeavor. Often, as we ascend the ladder of success, it is easy to forget how we got there, who helped us along the way, and who in fact secures our present position. However, these are dangerous facts to forget. Believe me, whoever you pass on the way up will be there to witness when you come tumbling down if you ever forget you are not your own source. It is by the grace of God and the support and kindness of others, coupled with honest preparation, that brings us to a place of success.

The additional value of befriending those who have not achieved or acquired what you have in your life is what keeps you innovative and sharpened. Those who are still striving to reach their destination are inspiring! They give fresh wind to tired wings. They are full of inventive ideas and passion. As you partner with them and assist them in moving forward, you will be filled with more creativity for your own life. It is the law of releasing energy; it feeds you with even more! Truly there is power in empowering others. Deborah was willing to be a leader to her people. She did not approach her job as a judge begrudgingly or behave as if she was doing anyone a favor. Her heart was with the people. They knew it and willingly followed her.

What principles can we draw from Deborah's story whether we are dealing with the man in our life, our friends, our children, family members, people in our place of business, or the world at-large? I think there are some golden nuggets here that can definitely leave us richer in spirit.

Diva Principles

First things first. Deborah had a kingdom-view of life. She saw the big picture. It wasn't about her. It wasn't about her personal world. It was bigger than that. It was about the greater good for all. Not only did she recognize the gifts in others, she saw their power and importance in the greater scheme of life. She did not allow Barak to remain dormant. She reminded him of his obligation to live up to the call on his life and encouraged him to move forward. She did not merely suggest. She followed through, willing to follow him to the battlefield to encourage him. This is big. Many of us

are simply too busy in our own worlds, with our own con-
cerns to stop and focus on others—yet it is imperative we
do. You see, if Deborah had let Barak slide, she, at some
point, would have been affected by his inactivity. The enemies of Israel might have become even more oppressive. As
the saying goes, "Evil flourishes when good men do
nothing."

She reminded Barak of his purpose in life and then got
him going. She didn't sit back and take for granted that he
could take it from there—no, she let him know she had his
back all the way. In true diva fashion, she was fearless and
extravagant with her support.

Diva Confession

*I will take the time to note the inherent gifts
of others and encourage them to live up to
their full potential. I will hold them
accountable and follow through with
them when necessary.*

With follow-through, you also have to know when to let
go and force others to spread their own wings. Deborah went
with Barak to the battlefield, but Mr. Man ultimately had to
fight his own battle. A selfish or insecure woman makes
others dependent on her strength so she will be important to
them. This renders the others powerless, stunts their growth,
and in the end completely paralyzes them.

Consider the example of the man who found a new butterfly struggling to crawl out of its cocoon. After carefully
cutting an opening and extricating the butterfly, this small

beauty died. Why? Because it is the struggle to get out of the cocoon that forces blood to pump through its veins and strengthen its wings. When robbed of the struggle, the butterfly died. And so do people. A diva lets a man be a man and knows her place as a woman. She does not see herself as insignificant or powerless. She is aware of her strength and what she contributes to the man in her life. She knows the importance of being a copilot—understanding that it takes two to fly, but one must lead. In terms of dealing with others, the same principle applies. Mastering the delicate balance of encouraging without rescuing allows others to exercise their inner being and grow in strength—empowered and liberated by their personal achievements.

Diva Confession

*I will be empowered as I empower others
to flourish in the area of their giftings.
I will not seek to control or even contain
them, but release them to their calling
with my blessing.*

When Deborah gave the marching orders to Barak, he was off and running, chasing the army of their enemies down until the battle had been won. True to Deborah's prophecy, however, Sisera died at the hands of a woman. Now can we talk about how this happened? As Sisera fled from the armies of Israel, he ran into the hands of yet another diva, Jael. Now Jael was a homemaker, seemingly harmless; however, the woman could pack a mean punch. After inviting Sisera in with the promise of refuge, she fed him some milk and as he drifted into an exhausted sleep, drove a tent peg into his temple and killed him. Who said homemakers are powerless and can't affect the world?

One of my mentors, Terri McFaddin, wrote a book entitled, *Only a Woman*. I second her motion—only a woman can win a battle without flexing a muscle, acting masculine, or making a big deal out of the fight. Certainly we have our own way of doing things. A diva knows how to win battles quietly. Notice where the damage was done. To his head. The mind. A woman can make or break a man by messing with his mind. This is why it is so important to harness our power and use it wisely. God holds us accountable for how we affect others with our words and our deeds.

Despite the fact that the glory of the battle went to a woman, Deborah still celebrated Barak's contribution in song as she retold the events of the victory. She kept his manhood intact and lifted him up among his peers. A true diva knows how to further empower those in her life by celebrating the offerings others make and magnifying even their small advancements to spur them on to greater heights. She is driven to draw the best out in others because she is aware of the fact that she is only as great as those who surround her.

Diva Confession

I will be a builder of confidence and not a destroyer of spirits. I will add and not subtract from the strength of others in my world. I will freely give praise and celebrate the fruitfulness of others.

Diva Do's and Don'ts

🍂 Seek to discover the hidden potential in others and encourage the use of their gifts.

🍂 Know when to encourage and when to release others to grow into the fullness of who they were created to be.

🍂 Speak the truth, but always with graciousness and gentility. The goal is to encourage positive action not paralyze.

🍂 Encourage even the smallest step, understanding that acknowledgement and praise can be the impetus for greater leaps in the future.

🍂 Do not seek to control, manipulate, or cause others to be dependent on you. This weakens you both in the long run.

🍂 Be driven to empower others—this is where true power lies. Remember, you are not a good physician if people keep having to come back to you.

🍂 Never consider someone beneath you. There is something to be learned and gained from every person we encounter. Who knows where they will be tomorrow?!

Div-otion

And let us consider how we may spur one another on towards love and good deeds (Hebrews 10:24).

Dear heavenly Father, make me an instrument of inspiration and blessing to others. As I empower others to fulfill their purpose, empower me to walk in the fullness of what You have created me to do and be. Amen.

Get Your
Heart
Together,
Sister!

Diva Profile

Ruth
(The Book of Ruth)

WHAT'S HER STORY:

She recovered gracefully from losses and was fruitful in spite of all she lacked.

INSIDE SCOOP:

From the land of Moab, a society of idol worshippers and very sensual people. She married Mahlon from Judah, son of Elimilech and Naomi. After the death of Mahlon, Ruth decided to follow her mother-in-law, Naomi, back to Judah. She became her caregiver, gleaning in the fields until discovered by the wealthy owner of the field, Boaz. She later married him and gave birth to a son who was the grandfather of David, king of Israel.

POTENTIAL WEAKNESS:

She could have become paralyzed by her loss. Fear of her future could have consumed her. She could have resigned from life after viewing her choices and finding the odds against her insurmountable. But instead, she chose to move forward.

STRENGTH:

The courage to begin again and trust God for a new beginning empowered her to move to Israel in spite of the threat of rejection she could face there. Her devotion and faithfulness to her mother-in-law caused her to give of herself sacrificially, and in the end God rewarded her richly.

DIVA-TUDE:

As Ruth's mother-in-law painted a bleak picture of her future should she choose to accompany her to Judah, Ruth was quick to say, "Entreat me not to leave you or to turn back from following after you; for wherever you lodge I will lodge. Your people shall be my people, and your God, my God. Where you die, I will die, and there will I be buried. The Lord do so to me, and more also, if anything but death parts you and me" (Ruth 1:16-17 NKJV).

THE TOUCH THAT MADE THE DIFFERENCE:

Her observance of her mother-in-law's faith while married to her son, Mahlon, must have had a profound effect on Ruth, persuading her it would be far better to try Naomi's God than stay behind and worship idols who did not answer. Somewhere deep within her being, she knew that if she wanted a different life she would have to do something different to lay hold of it.

The Endurance of a Diva

Whether we like it or not, even divas have storms in their lives. It's not the severity of the storm that you should be concerned about, but rather how you weather it. Hurt, betrayal, shattered dreams, and disappointments. Financial struggles, broken hearts, and losses are all a part of the cycle of life. Someone once said, "What doesn't kill you makes you stronger." How true! No one gets to be exempt from trials and troubles, but the response to hardship separates the girls from the women, the women from divine divas.

You can either embrace your pain and squeeze the life out of it, or give in to it and allow it to consume you. Yes, you do have a choice. I have found the most graceful people in life are those who have suffered through and endured many an ordeal. There is a sweetness of spirit, a solid grounding, an unshakeable peace that surrounds them as if to say, "Honey, I have been through worse. This, too, shall pass. Believe me." The resounding word that sums up their disposition is maturity. An integrity of soul that has been fashioned by the rough hands of life.

It is so easy to look at the shambles of our situation and be tempted to believe that nothing good could come of it. Worse yet, we believe there's no possible way the relationship or situation could ever be restored or repaired. But God is able to make something beautiful from the rags of our despair. To weave a rich tapestry that others behold and call beautiful. But this can only be accomplished by partnering with Him and making the right choices for moving forward.

Ruth found herself alone and broke after the death of her husband with no job, no home, no unemployment, and "no nothin'" as some would say. Talk about a legal reason to crumble and cry, but no! She resolved to remain in the land of the living and do it to the best of her ability. Fear of the unknown can be a daunting thing, making it hard to formulate any decisions or plans for the future. I believe Ruth had one thought in mind as she made her decision to go to Judah with Naomi and it was simply this: "I don't know what I'm going to do when I get there, but I know one thing, I'm getting out of here!" Sometimes you just have to launch out into the deep and trust God to catch you, my friend. What are your choices? Do nothing and *get* nothing or move forward and take a chance on something. Even if you get nothing, at least you took control of your destiny for one moment and tried. At least you now know what was on the other side of your question. For everyone I've ever known to take the leap of faith, they've found something better on the other side of their trouble.

A diva takes life by the horns and determines to ride until she is forced off. She does not volunteer to be a victim, but purposes at all times to absorb the shock of life's testing with dignity. No "why me" speeches are made. She understands the reality of life and chooses to live offensively rather than defensively. Never anticipating or walking in fear of trouble, but nevertheless knowing that it is inevitable in some respect. Therefore, she is prepared and ready to expedite recovery with as little dwelling on the negatives as possible.

Miss Ruth gives us so much to glean from her life story. Sound and profound advice for maintaining diva-hood even in the midst of trial.

Diva Principles

The first decision is usually the hardest. To shake yourself free from where you have been is always scary. I give Ruth a lot of credit. Because of her background she could have mastered all of the impossibilities for a new beginning in Judah. But instead, she chose to focus on the providence of God and step out in faith. Because she was from Moab she could not be sure how she would be received, according to Jewish law she should not be received at all. The Moabites were enemies of the nation of Israel. The Law stated that no Moabite could enter the assembly of the Lord...forever (Deuteronomy 23:3). They were so abhorred that the Jews were forbidden to even seek their peace or prosperity (Deuteronomy 23:6). So as you can see, Ruth was taking quite a chance by offering to accompany Naomi to Judah. But Ruth decided to cast her lot with God and move on His grace. He honored her belief in Him and surrounded her with graciousness that ended in rich provision in a strange land.

Naomi, even in the midst of grieving, was kind enough to consider the well-being of her daughters-in-law and offer them an out. (Ruth had a sister-in-law by the name of Orpah, who was married to Naomi's other son, who also died.) She told them their chances of finding husbands in Judah and remarrying were pretty much nil. On that note, Orpah went back home but Ruth persevered. This is where the famous wedding mantra originated, the whole "whither thou goest, I will go" speech. The bottom line here is Ruth wanted something different for her life. She refused to wallow in self-pity or remain stuck in her situation. She determined to get on with the business of living so she focused on a greater need than what she had herself—the needs of her mother-in-law. Naomi was old, alone, and would need someone to care for her on the journey back home as well as when she arrived. Focusing on someone else diminished Ruth's pain and here lies the first big secret...Get over yourself. The sooner you do, the sooner you will be able to see your situation in the right perspective. Once we have a realistic view of our circumstances, a solution usually comes to view. Even if it's nothing more than realizing the problem was not as overwhelming as it seemed in the light of someone else's greater distress. Looking beyond yourself is the first step to reaching the light at the end of the tunnel.

Diva Confession

I will not give in to the temptation to be self-consumed in times of crisis. Instead, I will focus on the needs of others less fortunate than myself and find healing in the giving of myself. In spite of my fears, I will be willing to step into the unfamiliar, believing God will meet me there and provide all my needs.

After making this bold step of faith, Ruth had another challenge to face: Survival. With no income, no supportive acquaintances, this was a serious situation. We don't know all of Ruth's background or the lifestyle she had been accustomed to in Moab. Perhaps she was a homemaker who had servants. Perhaps she had her own business on the side and did all right for herself. Perhaps life had been easy until her husband died. All of that was behind her now, and nothing could be considered beneath her as she and Naomi discussed amongst themselves what they could do to survive. Naomi must have brought up the option of gleaning in the fields and mentioned a relative who owned one. Ruth chose to make the best of their situation and work with what was available. She asked Naomi permission to go to that field to pick up leftovers from the harvesters citing perhaps because Boaz was a relative, he would be kind enough to allow her to work there. With Naomi's blessing, she went. Tirelessly, she worked without complaining to the point where she impressed the servants of Boaz with her countenance and diligence.

The point is not are we willing to humble ourselves in order to do what we must do to get through hard times, but what is our attitude as we do it. Life does not always serve us what we want on a silver platter, but the fact that we get served anything at all is reason enough to nurture a grateful heart and expect even greater things in the future. Nothing can change your circumstances faster than your attitude. After all, we never know who is watching. As in the case of Ruth, the coworkers were watching and were more inclined to be kind to her because of her attitude. Upon reporting all of this to Boaz after he inquired about her, he was moved to make extra provision as well as protection for her. Because we are not always aware of how God might want to bless us, or whom He chooses to bless us through, we must be cognizant of how we approach our circumstances. Greeting every opportunity, whether great or seemingly small, with a smile, an optimistic attitude, and graciousness to others sets the wheels in motion for someone to put in a good word for you in the right place and poof! Your situation can be turned around in a matter of fateful moments all because you continued to walk in grace—no matter how humbling your station or situation.

Remember, a queen is always a queen whether she has subjects and riches or not. She is a queen by birthright. What she has or lacks does not change her station in life. Reflecting on the story of Aida, the African princess that was kidnapped into slavery, the part that stands out in my mind was that her captor recognized that she was not just any old slave, even though she was dressed in rags. Who she was within literally transformed her appearance to those who had a discerning eye. There was no denying she was a princess. A diva is a diva whether broken or thriving, wealthy or poor. She will draw on the spirit of deliverance and break through because of the posture of her heart.

Diva Confession

I will not complain or be resentful
of my circumstances but will respond to
life and others with grace. I will glean
from what life has to offer me at the
moment, trusting God for increase as
I stay faithful in moving forward
one day at a time.

Well, time went by. Barley season and wheat season to be exact. Boaz had instructed Ruth to stay in his fields and not to wander off to others to glean. With no other agenda, Ruth focused on the task at hand, gathering enough to provide sustenance for her and her mother-in-law. Naomi was determined to bless Ruth for all she had done. She counseled Ruth that it was time she had some security in her life. It was time to take her relationship with Boaz to another level. In order to accomplish this, she must wash herself, perfume herself, put on her best garment, and go down to the threshing floor where Boaz would be after winnowing the barley. She was to take careful note of where he lay down, then lay at his feet and take the corner of his blanket and spread it over herself.

This was very significant. It was symbolic of asking the man to be her covering in marriage. She was to remind him that he was the next of kin to her husband and was therefore obligated to marry her to continue the family line and preserve their property. Ruth took Naomi's counsel and was richly rewarded for her obedience. Boaz did indeed marry her. Wow! This woman went from widowhood, to potential outcast, to gleaner in a field, to wife of a wealthy landowner! What was the common denominator throughout Ruth's entire journey? Acceptance with grace, humility, and faith. How dare she go to a town where she stood the chance of being thrown out or rejected? How dare she approach this rich landowner and tell him of her need for a redeemer? Only faith would dare to be so bold.

Even though vulnerability is a scary word for many women these days, it deserves a second look. Without noticing, the walls we put up to protect our heart and our expectations have made us unapproachable. Many an opportunity, willing helper, and even good man pass by staring at the invisible wall and fortress around us. All the while, the woman within those walls is crying out for someone to rescue her from her involuntary prison. Fear does a good job of convincing many that the only way to survive is to protect oneself. Which then makes us a prisoner of something we like even less—being alone.

Ruth dared to be vulnerable—knowing she had nothing to lose and everything to gain. And that is the bottom line. The only thing you have to lose is the fear of what would happen if you dared to reach out and let someone know your need. They can either say, "I cannot supply your need," which has nothing to do with you and everything to do with them. They can tell you how much of themselves they are capable or willing to give. Or, they can reach out and say, "I'm willing to give you what you need." Either way, you will know if you should pursue another avenue or not.

But let's get honest about why it is so difficult to ask for help. To be transparent in times of need. It is a greater giant than fear that looms behind the scene in our hearts. It is *pride,* which is actually a great deceiver. If you don't have what you need or want, then what do you have to be proud of? And why is pride necessary anyway? It always comes off wrong and does more harm than good. Taking "pride" in one's self usually leaves others assuming wrongly that we are arrogant, standoffish, and not in need of their attention or assistance. Nothing could be further from the truth. We see from watching any show on television, at the movies, and even from our day-to-day interactions that annoying woman we view as helpless. Really though, she's just being honest about her needs or shortcomings that always perpetuates someone running to her rescue!

Learn the lesson well. There is no crime or disgrace in being honest and asking for help. A diva is not humiliated by her needs, but rather is profoundly in touch with them. She makes no excuses about what she lacks because she understands that in God's economy He has made us all dependent beings. She realizes that pride will only rob her of vital relationships and opportunities for being blessed by the kindness of others. She values the gift of exchanging kindnesses and learns how to gracefully receive as well as give. She understands that allowing others to give to her is a way of adding value to their lives. She does not insist on an autonomous existence, but embraces the concept of community. Her relationships are transparent and open—sharing failures, needs, and fears, as well as victories and resources where needed. Accepting the cycle of having and not having as part of God's design for building character causes her to yield to times of difficulty devoid of complaints, knowing *this too shall pass*.

Diva Confession

I will not be a victim of pride losing more than what I presently lack when finding myself in times of need. I will graciously embrace the help that is offered me…seeing it as a gift from God as well as a blessing to the person reaching out to me and not view it as a confirmation of personal failure.

Diva Do's and Don'ts

❧ Allow times of testing and trial to deepen your character and beautify your spirit.

❧ Do not nurture self-involvement or pride when in a season of trial.

❧ Focus on the needs of someone you can help even in the midst of your test.

❧ Pursue change. If a different environment is needed to get past your situation, carefully consider moving.

❧ Do not move on impulse. Seek wise counsel before charting a new direction for yourself.

❧ Nurture a grateful spirit in the midst of your trials. Remember, there is always someone worse off than you.

❧ Be willing to do something you've never done before no matter how scary or humbling.

❧ Work with what you have at hand and trust God to increase it.

❧ Remain vulnerable and transparent with those that God places in your life. You never know which one of them could be your greatest source of blessing.

❧ Graciously receive help from those who offer, keeping in mind that the blessing is twofold.

Div-votion

Dear [sisters], whenever trouble comes your way, let it be an opportunity for joy. For when your faith is tested, your endurance has a chance to grow (James 1:2-3 NLT).

> *Dear heavenly Father, I will embrace every trial as an opportunity, knowing that it is working something out in me for the good, not just for myself but for the sake of others as well as for Your glory. Amen.*

Diva Profile

Abigail
(1 Samuel 25)

WHAT'S HER STORY:

She did not allow the foolishness of others to change her for the worse or rearrange her temperament.

INSIDE SCOOP:

Was married to a fool called Nabal. She was beautiful and sensible. He was mean and dishonest in all of his dealings. His refusal to give provisions to David's men who were on the run from King Saul of Israel almost brought ruin to his entire household. A servant escaped to inform Abigail that David's men were advancing against them in a murderous rage. Abigail quickly gathered resources and took them to David. She stood before him and fearlessly took the blame for her husband's foolishness and encouraged David to calm down and see the big picture. She urged him to consider his ways and how they might affect his future. He agreed with her and went peaceably on his way. After reporting to her husband what had happened, Nabal had a stroke and died. When David

received the news of her husband's death, he sent for
Abigail and married her.

POTENTIAL WEAKNESS:

When in the company of a fool, it is easy to act like a fool
yourself. Abigail didn't go there.

STRENGTH:

She was able to look past where she was and see the big
picture. She considered her actions and their lasting consequences before reacting on impulse.

DIVA-TUDE:

She was able to see the potential in David and remind
him of the future that God had promised him. She put his
present anger in the right perspective by telling him,
"When the LORD has done all he promised and has made
you leader of Israel, don't let this be a blemish on your
record" (1 Samuel 25:30 NLT).

TOUCH THAT MADE THE DIFFERENCE:

Her faith that God could and would change her situation
gave her infinite patience with a difficult husband, but
also kept her from reacting to his foolishness in a destructive manner.

The Character of a Diva

*F*ools! Can't live with 'em, can't kill 'em. Whether you like it or not, everyone you meet or have to deal with in life might not be of sound mind or character. So what's a diva to do when someone in her life is a fool? Whether it's your mate, boss, family member, coworker, the clerk at the checkout counter...whoever! You've got to maintain your diva-tude. Foolishness is a highly contagious disease because a fool can really make you lose your composure. There is just something about when a fool says or does the wrong thing to you. It's almost as if your brain shuts off and you become one major mass of reaction. A diva keeps her cool when everyone else is losing theirs.

Offense and embarrassment are two emotions that are highly combustible. It's natural to have a knee-jerk response and move to defend yourself, or to deflect an insult or accusation being thrown your way. There is no such thing as ducking these frustrations. No matter which way you turn, they land squarely in your heart. If allowed to remain, they fester and grow. They affect your mind-set, sprouting seeds of anger, despair, bitterness, and even foolishness on another level.

Don't go there! Whether the person in your life is abusive, insensitive, sarcastic, critical, or just plain doesn't think, one cannot fall prey to the madness. Stop, take a deep breath, consider your ways, and walk carefully. A calm, cool, and collected diva does not allow a fool to bring out the fool in her because she has replaced the seeds of foolishness in her own heart with divine wisdom.

A true diva masters the art of self-control. She exercises discretion and prudence, moving and acting carefully regardless of what is going on around her. She does not allow herself to be controlled by outer stimuli.

Let's talk about self-control and discipline for a moment. The world says do what you feel. But think about it. If everyone did what they felt like doing, or said what they felt like saying, we would all be in a state of constant chaos! The crime rate would be off the charts. Murder, robbery, embezzlement, oh my...not to mention adultery, rape, unwanted pregnancy...shall I go on? If everyone did as they pleased, there would be no end to the mass confusion and resulting pain.

Discipline is a necessary measure for order in the universe. Even nature operates by discipline. Things blossom according to their season. No bush or tree just *decides* to blossom when it feels like it—it has to wait for the fullness of its cycle to be completed. Rich fruit is produced when it comes forth at the right time; otherwise it is not good for consumption. It is useless.

Discipline comes from having understanding. Understanding of God's will and His way, as well as a profound insight into the consequences that foolish actions bring.

People cast off restraint when they have no understanding. These same people are known to wonder aloud why their life is filled with turmoil in the aftermath of their foolish behavior. Discipline and order are internal guidelines that make sure good fruit is produced in our lives. When good fruit is produced, it blesses not just the one who has grown it, but everyone who partakes of it.

I must confess that self-control does not always feel good initially. It could be declining a moment of temporary pleasure that could leave you with permanent baggage or scars. Or a moment where you would rather not be so diva-like. Let's be real…sometimes you just want to let it fly when someone insults or aggravates you. But when you consider what the fruit of that situation would be, wisdom assures you it would be far better to allow the other person to revel in their foolishness while you remain a mature observer. Satisfaction comes after the fact, when you are able to walk away with your dignity and your heart intact, assured of the peace that comes from making wise choices.

How does one master the art of self-control? First, honestly take stock of your weak areas. The things that make you snap or react, acting outside of divine character. Then make the decision to be disciplined in that specific area. It helps to know why you want or need to be watchful of your behavior or reactions. Decide the end result you would like in your circumstance or relationship. Is it peace? Then what is the best way to pursue peace in spite of what others around you are doing or saying? Does it pay to argue with a fool, to push their buttons, to defend yourself? Absolutely not. A fool is always right in their own eyes. Leave a fool to fight with themselves, focus on the positive, and refuse to absorb the negative. Miss Abigail specialized in this. Let's see what we can internalize as principles for being gracious under foolish fire.

Diva Principles

The first thing we must take note of is how Abigail is distinguished. The story recorded about her life in 1 Samuel says that she was beautiful and a woman of good understanding. Her husband, Nabal, on the other hand was a fool—harsh and evil in all his doings. She was able to maintain a reputation for wisdom and great poise even though she constantly dealt with a man who was insensitive, dishonest, and volatile. She was loved by her servants and her husband's employees and held in highest regard. From the details of how the story unfolds, obviously she had taken an honest assessment of her man and accepted him for who he was and learned how to work with him. She did not allow him to turn her into a fool or even the victim of one. Perhaps somewhere in her heart, she had an understanding of past wounds and disappointments that made him the man he had become. Perhaps when she regarded him, it was with pity and not resentment. Her ability to see his pain and lack of understanding enabled her to deal with him gently. The bottom line was…she did not take his foolishness personally and did not allow it to plant negative seeds in her spirit. There was no "the devil made me do it" attitude in her. She didn't need excuses for bad behavior because she chose not to bow to the temptation. Remember, no one can make you do anything. Whatever is in you will be projected outward.

Therefore, eliminate foolishness in your own heart and cultivate grace and wisdom.

Diva Confession

I will stay true to who I am, cultivating a gracious spirit even in the face of foolishness. I will consider the untold stories and weaknesses of others and cover them with grace.

We also need to investigate how Abigail was able to hold a confidence and not fan the flames of dissension. Her husband's employee felt safe running to her when Nabal jeopardized their lives with offending David, the upcoming king of Israel who was running from King Saul. When the servant gave her the report of the mess her husband had made, she did not defend his foolishness, nor did she confront it. Perhaps what the servant had said was accurate and she knew it, "You know no one can talk to him," he said. I can imagine Abigail thinking to herself, "You got that right!" but didn't say it out loud. First she calmed everyone down and then shifted into damage-control mode. Gathering supplies quickly, she mounted her donkey and went out to face David herself. When she reached him, she bowed to him and apologized on behalf of her husband, taking all the blame on herself! Now it takes *special* grace to do that. How quick we are to point the finger elsewhere, not wishing to have anyone sully our pretty dresses or our reputation. Casting the other person in a negative light in order to make ourselves look better comes a bit too naturally to most. She took honest stock of the situation and admitted that her husband was a fool. However, she covered him by inferring it was something he couldn't help, after all he was simply living up to his name which meant "fool." How can you blame a man for being a fool when, in a sense, his birthright promoted it?

The bottom line here is that many times, especially as women, we are quick to offer too much information in touchy situations that further fans the flames of strife. Abigail listened to the servant but did not feed on his negative information. Instead, she sought a positive resolution. When she reached David, she cited the reality of the offense and then went on to smooth things over by diffusing his anger. She diverted his attention back to what was truly important. He was to become king of Israel, he could not afford to have a fool make a fool out of him. There was too much at stake for his future. Consider the cost of a moment of foolishness versus maintaining your composure so that you walk into your destiny unfettered by regrettable past actions. She was able to make David see the light. He later commented on her wisdom.

It is far too tempting to nurse and rehearse the offenses and dealings of a fool, but to no productive end. It simply stirs up too much negativity in your own system. Part of disciplining yourself is learning how to be silent, refusing to give more acknowledgment to the offense. Foolish seeds that have been planted will wither and die if they have nothing to feed them. A diva only cultivates seeds that she knows will bear good fruit, and leaves the weeds to those who delight in tending them.

Diva Confession

*I will keep my eye on the big picture and
diffuse foolishness whenever it is in my
power to do so. I will not nurture
foolishness in my heart or in the hearts of
others but will seek to restore peace
wherever possible.*

Last but not least, Abigail resisted the urge to confront her
husband or lord her ability to fix things over him. When she
returned home, her husband was having a party. Can you
imagine? After the stress that she had just endured, it would
have been difficult not to interrupt his little celebration and
tell him what a fool he had been. But she kept her cool as
a true diva would. It was not important who had won the
battle...only that it had been won. The other component of
her ability not to confront and berate him was probably the
fact she knew in spite of what she said, he just wouldn't get
it. A fool always justifies his actions in his heart. So she
turned in for the night, left him to his revelry, and took time
to collect and center herself. The next morning over break-
fast she calmly related what had happened the day before.
Needless to say, as a natural fool would, Nabal had a fit.
Her response to his outburst is not noted; perhaps she had
none. All we know is that he had a conniption and literally
had a stroke over the whole thing. Ten days later he died!
When David found out about the death of Nabal, he sent for
Abigail to become his wife. She gracefully accepted his invitation. The moral of the story? Fools will always undo themselves when left to their own devices.

Diva Confession

*I will choose to master self-control in
my own life fully realizing the only person
I can control is myself. I will do what I can
do to maintain peace in my surroundings
and allow God to handle what I cannot.*

Diva Do's and Don'ts

⛆ Take honest stock of the person or situation you are dealing with and make no excuses for them.

⛆ Be sensitive to the weaknesses of others and ask God to give you insight into their actions that will help you extend grace to them.

⛆ Resist the urge to correct or berate a fool.

⛆ Focus on pursuing peace at all costs.

⛆ Remove yourself from people or situations that are not conducive to bearing good fruit in your life.

⛆ Do not repeat matters you experience or conversations you have with a fool. Others will not have the same measure of grace to forgive them. This will only prolong the offense in your heart as well as in the hearts of others.

⛆ Walk softly and consider all the facts before reacting or responding emotionally. Measure your words and choose wisdom.

❧ Take the time to really hear the heart of others when they speak, react, or even act out. Look beneath the surface of their actions and words in order to find some redeeming insight that will help you bear their outbursts with patience.

❧ When possible, cover the offense with grace and trust God to distribute justice on your behalf.

❧ Pray for and release your fool or situation, knowing that good always overcomes evil.

Div-otion

A wise man [woman] fears the LORD and shuns evil, but a fool is hotheaded and reckless (Proverbs 14:16).

Dear heavenly Father, help me to always walk in a way that is pleasing to You in spite of how I feel. Guard my responses to others who do not keep Your ways in mind. Amen.

Diva Profile

Mary, Mother of Jesus
(Luke 1:26-56; 2:19,21-35; John 2:1-12)

WHAT'S HER STORY:

She gave birth to Jesus, the Son of God, released Him into His destiny, and left a lasting legacy that touched the world.

INSIDE SCOOP:

Theologians estimate Mary was about fifteen when she experienced her visitation from the angel Gabriel. In the face of the enormous charge she had been given, she calmly considered all the options, asked the appropriate questions, and quietly yielded to God's plan for her life. Though being asked to be the mother of the Son of God was quite a lofty position, she considered herself a servant of the Most High and remained humble. She sought the wise counsel of her cousin Elizabeth who was also with child and acquiesced to her instruction. She pondered all the things she heard and saw in her heart. At the appropriate time, she released her son into the fullness of

His calling by encouraging His first miracle. She was present at His crucifixion and she was also present in the Upper Room, awaiting the visitation of the Holy Spirit after Jesus rose and ascended back to heaven. She went down in history as the one who was given the awesome title of "blessed and highly favored." The ultimate diva moniker.

POTENTIAL WEAKNESS:

Fear of public reaction to her pregnancy that had a rather dubious explanation could have made her not respond to the call of God for her life, yet she surrendered to His plan, trusting Him to work out the details.

STRENGTH:

She understood the depth of what she had been called to do, going against the natural instincts of a mother to cling to her child. She released her son to fulfill His purpose in spite of the pain it would cause her.

DIVA-TUDE:

After receiving the full impact of the message the angel Gabriel relayed to her from God, she humbly submitted to His will for her life and simply said, "Behold the maidservant of the Lord! Let it be to me according to your word" (Luke 1:38 NKJV).

THE TOUCH THAT MADE THE DIFFERENCE:

Her encounter with an angel and the subsequent touch of the Holy Spirit, who implanted a life in her that changed the course of the world.

The Heart of a Diva

*T*he greatest people in the world are those who don't know it. The biggest stars I've met were the most gracious people. Down-to-earth, over themselves, and went out of their way to treat those who were not as renowned as themselves with the greatest of kindness. Others I've met, who were up and coming, were completely egotistical and postured a poor imitation of how they thought true stars behaved. Self-importance has to be one of the most unattractive features a human being can ever display. Small wonder the Bible says that God gives grace to the humble, but resists the proud. The world has a negative response to those who are haughty and self-important, but the response to one who is humble (no matter how great) is always marked with warm respect and honest appreciation.

Divas have gotten a bad name in the past. They were seen as fabulous women who knew they were fabulous, swaying to the side of vanity and high maintenance. I maintain a truly divine diva is none of the above. She is a woman who knows that life is not about her, but rather the contribution she makes to others around her and the legacy she will leave behind. How will her life affect others? What other greatness can she birth beyond herself? How can she touch others in a lasting manner? What memories will she create throughout her lifetime in the hearts of others? What will she leave behind when she departs from a room or from this life?

Generally speaking, we spend way too much time living for ourselves, overlooking the power of sacrificial giving and living. We spend countless hours looking for ways to nurture self-improvement, but to what end? Are we seeking betterment for ourselves? Or are we seeking self-improvement so that we can better serve others? That is the big question.

It is true that we will never be able to love others if we don't love ourselves. However, many get stuck on loving themselves and never move beyond that. It's wonderful to feel good about you, but it is an even more incredible feeling to watch lives become transformed by your influence and efforts. It is sad to say that a lot of self-help books have merely made people prisoners of themselves, instead of liberating them to become greater contributors to those around them. The Bible tells us prophetically that in the last days, people will become lovers of themselves. Selfish and self-involved. And the love of many will wax cold. Small wonder so many are callous and uncaring, more concerned with being comfortable in their own personal space, fearing for their own comfort and safety when called out of their comfort zone to assist someone else in need.

And then there is Mary, the story of a young woman who should challenge us all. At such a young age, she accepted the awesome responsibility of bearing and nurturing the Son of God. Now many of you are saying as you read this,

"Come on, Michelle, that happened once in the history of the world. I doubt very seriously if there will be another Immaculate Conception. No one else will be asked to carry God's Son, so what's the point?" The point is we will not be asked to bear the Son of God, but we will be asked to bear something greater, the attributes of Christ. Which is where the word "Christian" comes from, meaning "imitator of Christ." It doesn't mean being a member of organized religion as some have been led to believe.

Yes, we are called to live for the needs of others and to lay down our life for them if need be. Not necessarily by going to the cross but by experiencing personal sacrifices of our own agendas and screaming desires. By reaching out to help someone when it is not convenient. Giving our lives by choosing to walk with someone who needs nurturing until their hidden potential comes to light. Being used as an instrument to leave a lasting impression and mark on the lives of others who need your special brand of love, wisdom, and finesse. You never know who you are truly dealing with. The person you speak a word of encouragement to could be the person who is elevated to a level where they affect countless lives. As divas, our influence is profound on those we choose to touch. We need to be more aware of our power and use it wisely and purposely.

Mary probably didn't think about all that I just mentioned when approached by her angelic visitor. She had such a vulnerable and tender heart toward God that when He called, she simply said yes. With one word, she becomes a stunning example of what true diva-hood entails. We can certainly learn from her simple but profound story.

Diva Principles

Despite the fact Mary already had plans for her life, she allowed them to be interrupted by God's plans. Just think, her life was tidy up to the moment the angel appeared. She was betrothed to Joseph the carpenter, it was simply a matter of time before they would be living together as husband and wife. She was a virgin, there would be no question of it on her wedding night. Life was good. Now, here stood an angel telling her she was going to be supernaturally impregnated by the Holy Spirit and would bear the Son of God! After asking exactly how this would take place and receiving an answer she probably didn't understand, Mary says yes to God's will without hesitation. Interesting...How did someone so young understand something so many mature folks still don't get? It wasn't about her. It was all about God and what He wanted to do with her life. She was His creation and handiwork. He could do with her as He pleased. She was His servant and that was a position of great honor. The privilege of serving Him surpassed any accolades she could earn for herself.

It was the dream of every woman in Israel to give birth to the Redeemer of the nation. I believe that carries into today...that men and women harbor a secret desire for greatness and the opportunity to make a lasting impact on the world. We all long to know our true purpose, to know we have made a difference in the world. That also seems to be a daunting thought. God is able to make each one of us uniquely powerful if we choose to submit to His design for our lives. What may seem small to you, might be a larger contribution to the world than you imagine.

How does one small child affect the entire world? He grows up and affects change in countless people—that's how. Mary had such a baby. In spite of the peril and disgrace she would have to face, she said yes to the angel's invitation. She risked the displeasure of her family, the gossip of neighbors, the possibility of Joseph divorcing her, and even being stoned to death for adultery. Not everyone will understand your purpose and call, but you must understand it and walk firmly in it. Mary said yes and didn't look back.

Diva Confession

I will stay sensitive to the voice of God and answer when He calls. I will seek the higher purpose for my life and be willing to sacrifice my personal agenda for the greater good of what I was created to do.

After the heady experience of an angelic visitation with such a profound announcement that she was "blessed and highly favored," Miss Mary could have gotten a big head. She could have felt that she was above counsel from anyone else because she could hear from God directly, yet that was not her attitude at all. She quickly made her way to the home of an older and wiser relative by the name of Elizabeth, who confirmed to Mary all she had already been told. There she remained to listen and learn from her older mentor in preparation for motherhood. Elizabeth was also giving birth to one who would later become John the Baptist—the man who would officially introduce Jesus to the nation. Together these two women shared natural and spiritual insights that fortified them for the births that would rearrange their lives in a way they could never have imagined. After receiving sound counsel from Elizabeth, Mary was ready to face marriage, motherhood, and a submitted life to God as she relied on His guidance to bring up this very special child in the way He should go. A diva understands the need for mentorship and sound counsel. She seeks it and embraces it, knowing that instruction is crucial to her success in fulfilling her purpose.

Diva Confession

I will be willing to receive sound counsel from others and yield to those who are able to nurture my gifts and guide me into the fullness of my potential. I will view them as instruments of God's hand sent to correct, exhort, promote, and provoke me toward my destiny.

Mary gives birth to Jesus in the humblest of places, a stable, and yet is visited by the greatest of men, three kings. They expound on the greatness of the child she has birthed and Mary ponders what they say. Some time later, she takes Jesus to the temple to be circumcised where they are approached by a devout worshipper of God, Simeon, and a prophetess called Anna. They both speak of the greatness of this child to all who will listen. This could have been pretty heavy stuff for an immature girl to handle, but Mary had become a woman. She harbored the secrets of God in her heart and did not feel the need to announce to the world any details about her miracle baby.

You see, a diva doesn't have to announce how great she is, or how marvelous her works are because these things speak for themselves. She did not seek special privileges but continued to live in a humble fashion, quietly raising her child to the best of her ability to follow after God. She allowed Joseph to lead her household and never considered him less spiritual than herself. She continued to be who she had always been—Mary, a woman sold out to God in thoughts, words, and actions. A true diva does not insist on special treatment or on having her own way.

Diva Confession

I will resist the urge to promote myself and allow my gifts and offerings to open the appropriate doors for me. I will concentrate on perfecting my gifts for the good of others and seeking the approval of God rather than the praises of the masses.

Then there was the wedding at Canaan. The scene of the first miracle by Jesus. At the wedding, the host ran out of wine. Mary tells Jesus about it only to be greeted with a "what do you want me to do about it?" attitude. But she doesn't let that stop her. In spite of His "my time has not yet come" speech, she instructs the servants to do whatever He tells them to and leaves Him to reconsider. There must have been something in her demeanor or tone of voice that caused Him to rethink His position and deal with turning the water into wine. Her quiet manner gave her son the quiet nudge He needed to step into the center of His destiny and begin fulfilling His calling. Nothing is recorded about her running around the wedding reception saying, "Did you see that? My baby turned water into wine!" No, none of that, just a quiet nod of approval from across the room I think, a special moment shared between mother and son. She had done her job well. She had raised her son to be ready for the world and then released Him to it.

Later she would experience the natural pangs that come when any mother has to release her children. For the sake of His ministry, Jesus' focus would shift to the needs of the masses, at times placing them above the needs of His own family. She would witness His crucifixion and death, and then have a short, bittersweet reunion that would never last long enough for her before He ascended into heaven. These were the moments that were prophesied to her, that a sword would pierce her heart and indeed it did. She bore these moments in quiet surrender to God's greater plan. She understood better than most the power of release. This was the ultimate test of her heart toward God. Could she surrender what was nearest and dearest to her for the greater good of others?

Mary's significance in this story is of huge importance to us. We become great when we birth greatness in others. This is how we build a legacy that lasts long after we have left this earth. One small contribution can have tremendous impact that resounds through the ages. It is not for us to know in the present. Perhaps we couldn't handle that much information. However, every woman, every *diva* should purpose in her heart to influence others to step into the fullness of their purpose and exercise their maximum potential.

Some, when launched into their destiny by your hands, will not look back. Don't consider it a thankless job when this happens. Know that your accolades come from a higher place. Take satisfaction at the fruit that is being produced.

A true diva is not interested in hogging the limelight. She is fiercely determined to *shed* light instead—the light of hope and the endless possibilities that come from nurturing the hidden gifts and talents of others until they become instruments of blessing in their own light. Ah…the feeling when your head hits the pillow at night because you've lived a day well-spent, affecting change or growth in the life of someone other than yourself. Influencer, inspiration, life-changer—these are titles that no one can tarnish or take away. Want to live the truly fabulous life? Then leave a lasting impression—sow seeds that won't wither but remain.

Diva Confession

I will not seek to become great, but will strive to birth greatness in the hearts of others. I will discard my search for temporary notoriety and seek to build a lasting legacy.

Diva Do's and Don'ts

෯ Nurture a sensitive spirit to the voice of God and a willing heart that responds to what He asks of you.

෯ Maintain a servant's heart no matter how great your position.

෯ Learn to allow His plans for your life to incubate in your heart. Practice the art of silence.

❧ Resist the urge to impress others with your blessings. Share with those who can rejoice with you and will offer sound counsel that keeps you on the right track.

❧ Discard all forms of selfishness. Cultivate a giving heart. Purpose to be joyfully sacrificial when the need arises.

❧ See everyone that God places in your life as a divine assignment.

❧ Take the time to identify and develop the hidden gifts and talents of others.

❧ Do not seek personal rewards or thanks from those you mentor. See their victories and achievements as your own and celebrate them.

❧ Do not envy the blessings of others. Rejoice in the diversity of gifts that God distributes in accordance with His divine wisdom. Learn to celebrate what you have received by sharing it with others.

❧ Recognize the season for every purpose and person that is placed in your life and be willing to lovingly release them when it is time.

❧ Look beyond the quest for personal satisfaction and embrace the greater fulfillment of depositing lasting treasures into the lives of others.

Div-otion

Whoever tries to keep his [her] life will lose it, and whoever loses his [her] life will preserve it (Luke 17:33).

Dear heavenly Father, help me to get over myself and concentrate on being a tool in Your divine hand for the greater good of others. As I plant seeds in the lives of those You have assigned to me, help me to yield a life and a legacy that You will smile upon. Amen.

Get Your
Life
Together,
Lady!

Diva Profile

Esther
(The Book of Esther)

WHAT'S HER STORY:

She mastered the art of being beautiful and getting a man's attention.

INSIDE SCOOP:

Orphaned at a young age, she was raised by her cousin Mordecai, during the time of the Jews' captivity in Persia. She was among those recruited to be considered for queen. Upon her arrival at the palace, she became the favorite of one of the head eunuchs, Haggai. Under his tutelage and special care, she blossomed into a rare beauty who learned how to dress for the part. She eventually was chosen by the king to become his next queen. After being crowned queen, she becomes privy to a plot by an evil man named Haman to exterminate the Jews. Her cousin beseeches her to intercede on her people's behalf to the king. She is reluctant at first because she has not been called for an audience with the king. According to the law, if she appeared before him without being called, she would be killed. Desperate, Mordecai persisted, convincing her that she must think beyond her personal security, suggesting perhaps her position as queen is not about her, but about a God-given assignment to save a nation. In the face of this bold and sobering statement, Esther takes courage and goes to face the king. After serving him and softening his heart with her ministrations, she wins the king's support and circumvents the plot against her people.

POTENTIAL WEAKNESS:

She could have become self-absorbed and cloaked behind the safety of her position, leaving her fellow countrymen to fend for themselves. She could have felt that she was above having to heed her older cousin's instructions and rebelled against authority, but she submitted to his wise counsel as well as God's direction.

STRENGTH:

She knew how to use what she had, a stunning combination of beauty and wisdom, to get what she wanted. Her humility and willingness to listen to and heed wise counsel was the stepping-stone to promotion in her life.

DIVA-TUDE:

After being challenged not to settle into her position for her own personal glory, she decided to step outside her comfort zone and do whatever it took to save her people. The depth of her conviction was clear as she declared, "If I perish, I perish."

THE TOUCH THAT MADE THE DIFFERENCE:

The counsel of her cousin instructing her to look beyond the fabulous glitz and sumptuous lifestyle of the palace and focus on her purpose had a resounding effect on her view of life and how she was to live it.

The Posture of a Diva

irst impressions are lasting ones. For most opportunities in life, you've got exactly one shot to get the attention of the powers-that-be. This being the case, you've got to "come correct" as they say in Urbanese. There can be no apologizing for your appearance with the assurance that, "I clean up well, trust me." Nope, you've got to be ready for prime-time TV when the lights go on. When opportunity meets preparation, things happen—doors open, favor is released, and promotion is extended to you—if you know how to dress for the part. Every diva knows in order to win friends and influence people, she must put her best face, as well as foot, forward. Though God looks at the heart, people look at what is obvious to the eye. The reality of everyday living is appearance is important and must be mastered in such a manner that your true character outshines your exterior. Your exterior should complement the true beauty that comes from within.

Now there is a way to dress and *a way to dress*. Dressing to perfection begins, first of all, with preparation of the body followed by the right foundation. When I was a child, my mother preached the virtues of cleanliness citing that to put a beautiful dress and perfume on a dirty body was like putting icing on gingerbread. No matter how sweet the topping, the taste of the ginger would cut through. The same is true for inner attitudes—funky dispositions, bitterness, or vanity—I don't care how fabulous the dress, it can't possibly cover all of that. We're going to deal with dressing on all levels—from the inside out.

Dressing must begin beneath the surface. Whatever is going on inside you is sure to shine through and overcome your accessories if not dealt with. Small wonder Esther and the rest of the candidates for queen of Persia were put through such a rigorous beauty regime before having any contact with the king. Let's discover together what we can learn from our sister Esther on the art of being so fabulous that the hearts of many are won, including a king or two!

Diva Principles

When the search was launched for the next Mrs. Persia, one of the requirements was virginity—which was proof of purity back in the day. However, we know purity is a much deeper issue. A woman can be a virgin but still not be pure of heart. She might have mastered self-control in one area of her life but has allowed her heart to run amuck. She might be self-righteous, bitter, or covetous...all the while justifying her bad behavior because she's done one thing right. This does not a pleasant person make. On the other hand, you can meet a woman who has made her mistakes, is well aware of them, and walks in humility and purity of spirit because she has had a change of heart concerning the way she wants to live her life.

Purity of heart is a beautifier no one can ever bottle and sell. Purity of heart keeps one's agendas on the right track and is followed up with pure actions that are pleasing to man as well as to God. Purity of heart puts a sparkle in the eyes that no bottle of Visine could replicate. It will also help you to avoid circles under the eyes from lack of sleep because a pure heart is able to rest well with a clean conscience. Hidden agendas, undercover motives, sneakiness, and manipulation are all toxic energies that mar our natural beauty. Avoid them like the plague. True divas walk in grace because they embrace the power of being pure in heart. They leave no doubt in anyone's mind that they harbor only the best of intentions. Everyone they meet is liberated to embrace them without reservation.

Diva Confession

I will keep short accounts of offenses and seek to keep my heart and lifestyle pure. I will be the sentry of my heart condition and will not fall prey to self-righteousness or comparing myself to others. I will approach each person in my life without guile or hidden motives.

Hmm...the next thing I find interesting in Esther's beauty regime is the fact she was given special quarters apart from where the other candidates and concubines were lodged. There is something to be said for being set apart. A diva guards her heart and mind wisely. She does not associate with others who are competitive, those who entertain constant drama in their lives or harbor negativity. She sets herself apart and enjoys solitude, knowing this is where nourishment for the soul is found. She makes time for herself, *by* herself, in order to listen to the still, small voice of God and renew her mind and soul. It is in the quiet times truths come to light. Solitude is vital to anyone who wants to keep their mind clear, their body rested, and all their mental faculties on point. All the various external voices that pull us this way and that must be eliminated for a time in order to hone in on important personal truths.

Take the time to commune with God and yourself in order to hear the things that will keep you in perfect peace. Peace within translates outwardly as serenity, which others find attractive and are drawn to. This is an important step to putting your best face forward. True divas welcome the alone times as they would an oasis in the desert, knowing this is where true refreshment and soundness of mind is found.

Diva Confession

I will guard my heart and mind against all negative and unhealthy associations. I will welcome moments of solitude and make them my friend. I will take the time to silence all noises that could distract me from the still, small voice of God.

Also critical to Esther's beauty regime was her diet. Ow! I know no one wants to go there but we must. What we eat has lasting effects on our health, as well as our beauty. Obviously Haggai, the eunuch who oversaw her beauty treatments, was well aware of the cosmetic effects of food on the skin, figure, weight, and even mental clarity. If we are what we eat, then truly most of us are in trouble! Diet is a very personal choice. We all get sick and tired of being sick and tired of how we look and feel. Sometimes that's what it takes in order to make the necessary changes for our well-being. The prophet Daniel, when taken away to Babylon, was very cognizant of his diet even though he had access to all the delicacies that were served in the palace. He refused to defile himself with the sumptuous fare that was put before him and opted instead for a balanced diet of fresh fruit, vegetables, grain, and water. After several weeks, his mental acumen soared above the other young men who had been recruited to be in the king's service (Daniel 1–2). What we eat affects us more than we realize.

Recently, after battling with sudden weight gain, bouts of forgetfulness, as well as various aches, pains, and health issues, I went to visit a nutritionist. What he told me was shocking! Though I forgot to eat most of the day due to my rigorous schedule, when I did finally eat, no matter how small the portions I was eating, I gained weight. Why? Because what I ate was not compatible with my system. My body was not processing the food properly, turning it into acid which was causing me major discomfort. Or, it was storing it as fat instead of eliminating it. I felt sluggish and tired all the time, coupled with a multitude of other symptoms that threatened my energy level and productivity. I didn't like my appearance at all and I looked as bloated as I felt. After realigning my diet to his specifications, the weight fell off, I had more energy, I felt great, I looked great, and my mind was restored to mental sharpness. People noticed the difference and my self-confidence soared. I was even able to get into clothing I had only gazed at longingly as it hung in my closet.

Can everyone be a size two? No. It might not even be your preference. Being tiny should not be the ultimate goal. Eating properly to become and stay healthy should be. Feeling good and up to peak performance. Being strong and fit, not plagued by sluggishness, dullness, aches, and allergies. According to experts, if you grow sleepy after eating, you are overtaxing your body with things that are hard for your system to break down and absorb. If you eat sparingly and still struggle with your weight, I would encourage you to check out some books on how to eat according to your blood type, as well as food combining. Though it might not work for all, it has certainly worked for me.

You have to be honest with yourself. Is your diet healing you or killing you? Do you like the way you look and feel right now? If you knew what you were about to put in your mouth was laced with poison, would you eat it? Then why do we eat things we know are not good for us or beneficial to our outward appearance? What other void are you attempting to fill with food? I suggest you deal with your issues and give your body a break. It's the only body you have, be kind to it. Take care of it and it will work for you for a very long time. Make it a life-goal to eat a healthier diet. Decide no matter how tempting those tasty morsels look, you will resist the urge to partake if they are not good for you.

I would like to challenge you to do a Daniel fast for 21 days to cleanse your system and help you get on the right track to a healthy body. That would be fresh fruits, vegetables and water. That's it. No potatoes, rice, bread, or meat. No dairy. No sugar. If you must have something hot you may steam your vegetables, but try to stick to raw for fiber. I'd love to hear from you to let me know the results. You will be amazed at how much energy you will have and how much better you will feel. Consult your physician before beginning this fast as you would with any health-maintenance program.

Though we have desires, they should not rule over us. Divine divas practice self-control in this critical area and make whatever investment they have to in order to walk in soundness of mind and body. In short, they take care of themselves. We spend so much money covering up our bodies, how about investing in your body's well-being? If you've come to the conclusion that you have not been taking the best care of your temple, will you join me in this prayer?

> *Dear heavenly Father, I long to be a beautiful vessel that reflects the glory of Your handiwork. Please forgive me for not taking good care of the body You have given me. As I purpose to set boundaries that protect my well-being, as well as the gift of beauty that You have given me empower me to make the right choices concerning my diet. Help me to resist temptation in the areas of overeating and impulsively eating things that are not good for me. Fill the voids in my heart I attempt to fill with food and restore my sense of healthfulness. In Jesus' name I pray, amen.*

Diva Confession

I will be kind to my body and nurture it to be the best that it can be. I will no longer eat out of emotion but will make wise choices and select food that will promote my health, strength, and beauty. I will be as discriminating about what I put into my body as well as what I put on it.

No, I'm not finished. Just as certain foods we eat cause our bodies to work harder than it should, we physically drive ourselves into the ground as well. America is a country that suffers from over-stimulation. Most people would say they are overworked and underpaid, yet we remain a driven people. While Europeans insist on five to six weeks of vacation a year, most of us could never imagine being away from work that long even if we would like to be. We say we cannot afford to take that much time away from our duties, real or imagined. The truth of the matter is we can't afford *not* to rest. Esther was given all types of healing baths and massages with precious oils. The theory behind massage is relaxation—releasing tension and toxins from the body that can poison the system and result in pain and stiffness. Stressed muscles and joints can affect our posture as well as our facial expressions. You must find out what promotes rest and relaxation for yourself and make sure you indulge in it.

If God took the time to rest and celebrate His creation, shouldn't we follow His example to call all activity to a halt and rest? Whether it's a bubble bath, a walk through a park or a day at the spa, choose your form of rest and be faithful to take the time you need in order to restore your soul, as well as your body. Stress, tension, and being overworked are sure to mar your countenance and cause others to voice their concern. "You look tired...are you all right?" Not exactly the results you want after working so hard on your appearance.

Rest is not just a physical issue. Rest must be achieved on all levels in order for you to function and look your best. Spiritually, emotionally, mentally, and physically. On the spiritual note, there are two different types of rest. First, peace with God removes the stress of a conscience burdened with shame, pain, and secrets. Take the time to come clean with Him through confession and repentance (your willful decision not to repeat your mistakes), to accept His grace and mercy. To rejoice in the gift of eternal life that Jesus Christ provides and know that all is well with your soul. Second, knowing that God will take care of the things that overwhelm you is a big relief. He urges us to cast all of our worries on Him because He cares for us. Trusting Him to be present and caring about every issue of your life releases you from stress and worry.

Emotional rest is just as vital to your beauty regime. Unload any emotional baggage from toxic and unhealthy relationships—whether familiar, platonic, or romantic. Set healthy boundaries to protect your heart from anxiety, fear, and worry. Mentally, learn how to disconnect from your work once you leave it or any stresses that burden your mind for way too long. Relax and release. For me, a funny novel or television show becomes my escape. A good laugh helps me to release things I continue to process over and over again. I find solutions come easier after I've divorced myself from continually nursing and rehearsing whatever situation I'm concerned about. Find a way to hit the off button in your mind and refuse to overthink issues. They often resolve themselves after you let go of them anyway. Take a mental health day. Stop and take the time to think about absolutely nothing. Even a mind needs to be emptied every now and then to make room for greater thoughts.

On the flip side of rest is that most dreaded subject—exercise. I promise to keep it short. In this area, women seem to run the gamut with two extremes, those who are obsessed with it and those who do nothing at all. The key here is balance. The reality of life is, as most of us grow older, our metabolism will need us to partner with it to keep it going. All I ask is that you do something!

Walking is one of the most wonderful ways of staying fit. Get out and take a good-paced walk through the neighborhood, through the park, along the lakefront, around a large parking lot, or wherever—just get out and get that blood pumping. If you need a little extra incentive, invite a friend to partner with you and make it a time of reflecting and praying together. I did this with a girlfriend one summer and went down two dress sizes! My day went better because it started with a stimulating conversation about the Word. We would each share what scripture was on our hearts and what we got out of it. By the time we were finished, the hour had fled by, we were refreshed in our spirits, and our bodies were revitalized with an abundance of energy. The rest of the day seemed to peacefully fall into place every time we purposed to start our day this way. If you need extra help and can afford it, enlist the help of a physical trainer to map out a program for your specific needs. Decide what works best for you, what you will be consistent with, and go for it. It can even be an exercise video you can do in your home, just do something. Exerting energy releases more energy so push yourself until you feel your energy level rising. Your heart will thank you for it, as will the rest of your body. When your body feels good, it will look good. And when you look good you will feel better about yourself.

Now can we talk about those who are addicted to over performing? Constantly being on the go does not add up to good exercise. It adds up to high stress levels that cause the body to rebel against us. Everything from glandular problems to fibroids to a host of other common "female problems," are now being attributed not just to our diets but our heightened stress levels. Our bodies are pleading with us to slow down and yet many are guilty of ignoring the warning signs. Believe me, if you do not listen to your body, it will still have the last say. Stop! Breathe in, breathe out, and sit down. Put your feet up. Enjoy a moment of silence and doing absolutely nothing. Pay attention to how much sleep your body says it needs and learn to say a very small, but difficult word, "No." No to the constant invitations and activities that all sound good. When done continually, these activities and obligations wear you down and make you a very unpleasant person with shorter and shorter amounts of patience. In all things, pursue peace. Peace for your mind, peace for your emotions, peace for your spirit, peace for your body. Make discerning choices about what you say yes to and consider their long-term effects. Ask yourself: Is this something that is going to wear me out? Or make me wonder later why I agreed to do it? If the answer to both of those questions is yes, you need to learn to shake off the bondage of false obligation—making everyone happy except yourself—and say no. Take the time to love yourself and you will find it easier to love others. And guess what? They will love you back. It is vital that you make a daily effort to nurture your body, mind, and soul.

As nurturers, we often find it difficult to ask for help—even if we desperately need it. Esther was given seven maids to assist her. Women find it hard to admit when they need help. We are the masters of multitasking. Many would never voice out loud they are resentful after saving the day for countless others. Overextended and underappreciated, they crawl into their beds at night wondering why no one ever comes to their rescue. Never admitting that their addiction to caregiving is in overdrive, they literally push themselves to the brink of exhaustion and then blow up, much to the shock of their inner circle who assumed they enjoyed helping everyone. Sound familiar? It's time to get real about how much you are really capable of. Go ahead, admit it, "My name is not Superwoman!" Stop the madness of overextending yourself. Divas know their physical limitations and take the time to rest. They have no problem asking for help when they need it and saying no when a yes won't do anyone any good. They are forever cognizant of nurturing their well-being, knowing ill health would render them ineffective, unable to do anything for themselves as well as others. One of the greatest gifts you can give yourself is the knowledge of when enough is enough.

Diva Confession

I will no longer be unrealistic about my physical limitations. I will take the time to rest and renew myself so I can be of better service to others as well as myself. I will be honest about my needs and seek help when needed. I will value myself and nurture my health and well-being.

Now we get down to the nitty-gritty. The stuff that we usually think of first when it comes to beauty—hair, makeup, and clothing. When the time came for Esther to have her audience with the king, she was given the opportunity to dress and accessorize herself any way she wanted to. Many candidates had gone before her, dressing as they always had, only to find themselves rejected by the king. However, Esther didn't go on her own personal knowledge or past habits, she asked the king's right-hand man how she should dress. By the time he was finished selecting her wardrobe and directing her overall toilette, she was the rave of the court. Now I realize most women don't have the budget to employ a personal clothing stylist, but a little wisdom can go a long way.

First rule of thumb: Divas *set* fashion trends, they don't follow them. Classic, simple, and complementary are the key buzzwords when referring to how a divine diva dresses. Always in good taste, never outshining the person who is wearing the garment. Divas dress in a way that causes others to look twice, though nothing they are wearing is screaming for attention. It's the color, the fabric, the fit that accents a woman's best features and appropriately minimizes anything that should not warrant extra consideration. This type of dressing can be achieved at any price point. Whether you shop at Marshall's, T.J. Maxx, Target, WalMart, Saks Fifth Avenue, or Neiman Marcus, the same high-level look can be achieved. It's simply a matter of taste and some discerning choices about fabric and cut. When in doubt, ask someone who is considered a good dresser for advice.

Invest in a basic wardrobe that can be dressed up or down with accessories, while paying strict attention to the fact that less is more. Don't be afraid to pay slightly more than you are used to for your basic pieces. Pay attention to fabric content. Pure fabrics last longer than blends. When you consider how many times you have to buy the same inexpensive white blouse over and over again, you could have bought a slightly pricier blouse that would have lasted a lot longer. The same goes for that basic black dress, skirts, slacks, and blazer. Choose a color palette that easily coordinates. You should be able to interchange all of your pieces with one another unless you are not on a limited budget and have an extensive wardrobe. Classic cuts lend themselves to weathering the test of time. They are never out of style and they always look good. I know I don't have to tell you this, but there are some who need to know—be honest about what size you wear and purchase accordingly. Well-fitting garments (that means not too tight) always look better. Find a good tailor and have them custom fit your blazers to compliment your figure. You'd be amazed at what a couple of darts can do to a simple jacket.

Being an educated shopper can make the difference between a mediocre wardrobe and a fine one. For those who love to purchase jewelry, most cities have jewelry districts where pieces can be purchased wholesale. Most jewelry stores are also open to negotiating price. You should always ask them for the best price they can offer on the piece that you are considering. Be willing to take the time to bargain with them, you would be surprised at the savings you will reap. I once got a piece of jewelry at a store in New York for a fourth of what they were originally asking. It took me 40 minutes of haggling, but I walked away just as delighted with what I spent as what I had acquired. Compare prices for similar pieces to make sure you are getting a good deal before making a purchase. Learn about the things you want to purchase; know what you should be looking for and the average prices in order to make wise decisions.

Choose your accessories carefully—they should never overpower your outfit. Accessories were created to complement your outfit, not distract from it. Resist the urge to buy a bunch of fussy costume jewelry. One real piece of jewelry goes a long way. When dressing to impress, true divas keep it simple and real. Try saving up some of your shekels and treat your clothing and jewelry as investments. Investments in your image. What you wear says a lot about you. What is the impression you would like to leave behind? Well then, present that image going in.

Since we are on the subject of putting your face forward, let's discuss makeup for a moment. Makeup should be an enhancer, not a mask. When in doubt, you can enter a department store and have a makeup technician do a free beauty makeover. Ask them to show you how to apply makeup that works for day and evening. One should be a classic, natural look and one should be slightly more dramatic. Take care in matching skin tones and find one that looks natural. Select shades of eye shadow, blush, and lipstick that are soft and match with your skin tones. Avoid harsh lines around the lips, eyes, and brows. Take the time to blend your colors so that there is no obvious beginning or end to them. Brows should have a natural arch—always wax or pluck from underneath, not on top! Careful trimming may be required to even the shape on top but follow the lead of what is naturally there. There is no excuse for bad makeup today because of all that is available.

We can't have your face and body together and ignore your hair. Your hair should work for you, not against you. It should be a flattering frame for your face and should not distract from it. Whether you choose to go *au naturale* or add extensions, the same rule applies, keep it simple. Follow the natural tendency of your hair and learn to work with it. Some people spend their entire life fighting against the natural state of their hair and never seemingly win the fight. Straight, wavy, nappy, it's all good. Find a place of comfortable practicality and cultivate it. The first thing is always a good cut. Followed by a complimentary hair color. If doing highlights, stay away from dramatic transitions. Hair, even when done, should never look *done*. In other words, it shouldn't look as if it took a lot of effort to achieve the beautiful you. Transition your different hairstyles gradually, the shock factor is never good for you or those around you.

Find a hairdresser you like and stick with that person. Experimenting with different hairstylists can be dangerous. Find one who will learn your head, understand what your hair needs, and nurture it to its fullest potential. If you are good at doing your own hair, then perhaps you only need someone to lay the foundation for you with a good cut. Vidal Sassoon has long been a staple for the perfect precision cut; no matter which way you turn, your hair will fall in place. I can hear people screaming "I don't have Vidal Sassoon money!" Yes, you do.

Here's a little diva secret for getting some of the extras you may need. Every time you break a dollar bill and receive change, throw it in a money bottle in your room. You will be amazed at the end of the month how much money you have! Where there's a will, there's a way. We all seem to find money for what is truly important to us.

Have I covered everything? Oops...two last, but important features. First, the scent of a woman should always be intriguing and alluring. Find an oil, parfum, or *eau de toilette* that is distinct. Don't select a fragrance on the first spray. Spritz it gently on a pulse point and walk around for a bit until it has had a chance to dry and mingle with your personal chemistry. Pick a fragrance that is you. Warm or fresh. With deep undertones or the smell of fresh flowers, each makes a personal statement about who you are. Never overdo your fragrance. You want people to draw closer, not be repelled. And when you exit, it should softly linger and leave a pleasant memory. There are some people in my life that I associate strongly with scent. Whenever I come into contact with that particular smell, I think of them and it makes me smile. Choose your scent carefully.

Last, but not least, your feet. Taking care of your feet is important. After all, they support the rest of your being. The choices for shoes are endless, but choose wisely. Lovely, but comfortable, is the best route and still gives you countless options. Buy shoes that don't throw your posture out of line and you can walk gracefully in. Pick shoes that compliment the line of your legs. Know the difference between shoes you wear with slacks and dress shoes. No matter what, get regular pedicures to keep feet attractive and callous-free.

Always dress from the top of your head to the tips of your toes as if you are one complete picture, then select the profile you want to present. Everything should work in harmony to put you in the best light. Classic, phenomenal, feminine, and so you! Understated, but definitely saying something as only a diva could.

Diva Confession

*I will consider beauty an art to be
mastered on all levels and act accordingly.
I will not be a follower but a leader of
trends. My appearance will frame and
compliment my spirit, not distract from it.*

Diva Wardrobe Rules

% Always build your basic wardrobe with neutral colors, then add more vibrant shades for accents.

% Wear dark colors on areas you don't want to draw attention to.

% To look taller, wear a monochromatic outfit.

% When wearing all the same color, add interest by wearing different textures.

% Dress to accentuate the positive and minimize the negative areas of your body.

% Accessorize to compliment, not distract.

Diva Shopping Secrets

% Summer designer-priced merchandise usually goes on sale the first week of June. Winter markdowns begin on fall merchandise the first week of December. Make sure you catch the largest discounts during the last markdowns at the end of July and January.

❧ Always check the newspapers for additional markdown coupons or ask your salesperson for them.

❧ Make friends with a salesperson at the stores that you regularly shop in. Make them familiar with your personal style. Ask them to call you when the things you like go on sale. This is the biggest rule for shopping. Never pay full price.

❧ If you've bought an item that has gone on sale the week after you purchased it, if you still have your receipt, most stores will honor the sale price and give you back the balance you should have saved.

❧ For cosmetics, there are many brands that give you high-end results—L'Oreal, Revlon, and for those with sensitive skin there's Almay and Neutrogena. Of course we can always rely on Maybelline for the best mascara. For women of color Black Opal, Posner, Flori Roberts, and Iman cosmetics have some of the best colors on the market. Fashion Fair was there when no one else was and continues to update their line and colors.

❧ For those who prefer to shop at department stores for their makeup Mac, Bobbi Brown, Prescriptives, Lancôme, Estée Lauder, Clarins, Laura Mercier, and Clinique have long been favorites for a good reason. They offer a wide selection of shades and colors to match and compliment your skin along with great skin care items.

Diva Don't-Miss-Sale List

℀ Neiman Marcus—Last Call sale for one week mid-summer, and winter semi-annual events.

℀ Saks Fifth Avenue—Semi-annual clearance in January and July.

℀ Marshall Field's—Field Days is held several times a year. A 90 percent designer-wear markdown the beginning of February.

℀ Bloomingdale's—Semi-annual sales in early January and the end of August. Extra markdowns begin in July and December.

℀ Nordstrom—Half-yearly sale in June and November.

℀ Macy's—Semi-annual storewide clearance in early January and the end of August.

℀ T.J. Maxx—Markdowns of 60–70 percent throughout January and July. Tons of fabulous finds.

℀ Target and WalMart—You're sure to find great prices on basics as well as a variety of personal grooming products, makeup, and household needs any time. Two of my favorite places.

Diva Do's and Don'ts

℀ Never believe a great outfit can make up for a horrible disposition.

- Avoid trendy pieces and cheap imitations. Keep it real and classic.

- Find the look that's great for you and stick with it. Make transitions gradually as you mature.

- Do not experiment with your hair. Think of those classic divas such as Jackie O, Audrey Hepburn, Sophia Loren...their hair was a part of their trademark. Your hair identifies you, don't allow others who have nothing invested in you to rearrange you.

- Keep in mind, it's the little things that complete your toilette. A good manicure and pedicure. Finished brows, clean skin, and the proper foundations under your clothing. Divas do wear slips! They know the power of leaving something to the imagination.

- Don't buy things at the original price unless they are so classic you can justify the expense because of the wear you will get out of the piece. This only applies if you feel the piece will not make it to sale time. When in doubt, ask the salesperson in that department.

- Keep a list of the pieces you need for your wardrobe. Don't buy things just because they are on sale. Buy them because they are a needed addition to what you already have.

- If unsure of the image you would like to present, consider some classic divas that look like you. Select a look or example you are comfortable with, then cultivate and personalize it.

❀ Look complete but not overdone. It should never look as if you tried too hard to achieve your overall appearance.

❀ Remember at all times that clothing does not make the woman, it merely reflects the lady within.

Div-otion

Your beauty should not come from outward adornment, such as braided hair and the wearing of gold jewelry and fine clothes. Instead, it should be that of your inner self, the unfading beauty of a gentle and quiet spirit, which is of great worth in God's sight (1 Peter 3:3-4).

> *Dear heavenly Father, help me to remember that I am a reflection of Your handiwork at all times. Guide me and help me to take proper care of the vessel You have created. Help me to wisely display it in a fashion that will reflect the beauty You've placed within me and will bring honor to Your name. Amen.*

Diva Profile

Lydia
(Acts 16:11-15, 40)

WHAT'S HER STORY:

She mastered the art of balancing success and prosperity in the secular marketplace with a profound devotion to maintaining her spiritual beliefs and ethics.

INSIDE SCOOP:

Lydia, a single Greek woman (possibly widowed), was reportedly a wealthy owner of a business that traded in an exotic purple dye and fabrics at Phillipi, a bustling trade route located in a Roman colony. She was a woman of prayer who, upon meeting Paul, received further instruction in the ways of the Lord, was baptized, and then opened her home to Paul and his missionaries. She is noted as being the first named convert to Christianity in Phillipi and for hosting the first church in Europe in her home.

POTENTIAL WEAKNESS:

Her prominence and profitable trade could have pulled her in the same direction other successful women of her day were drawn to. They used their economic power and influence to further their social and political ambitions. Lydia did not believe the hype or get caught up in it. She rejected the idols they worshipped to bring prosperity to their businesses and wasn't involved in their cliques. Instead, she turned her attention toward God and helping His people.

STRENGTH:

She had the courage to walk against the flow of the society she lived in and pursued her own spiritual agenda. As a woman of prayer, she was discerning of the true purpose of her wealth and holdings. On the basis of this revelation, she gave her best back to God and His people.

DIVA-TUDE:

After being baptized by Paul, she knew this was just the beginning of God's plan for her life and chose to embrace her destiny as she pleaded with Paul, "If you have judged me to be faithful to the Lord, come to my house and stay" (Acts 16:15).

THE TOUCH THAT MADE THE DIFFERENCE:

After Paul arrived on the scene teaching her and her other prayer partners things they had long wanted to know but had no access to, she received the full impact of the Gospel message and was baptized.

The Power
of a Diva

W e all crave power. Perhaps it is part of our spiritual makeup because our heavenly Daddy is all
powerful. God desires for us to have it, too. He
gives us the power to gain wealth. However, He expects us
to be wise stewards of what He gives us. It is never His
intention or desire that the gifts we receive would replace
the Giver.

In today's fast paced world, it is easy to get caught up in
all the trimmings. It seems the capacity to gain great wealth
only ignites the passion to reach for even more. It becomes
a vicious cycle. A raise on the job means we need a bigger
house, which then requires new furniture, a better car to sit
in the driveway, better clothes to ride in the car, and on and
on. Before you know it, we become masters of consumption—to bless ourselves and further our own personal
agendas. All the while, God had a completely different idea
in mind when He handed us all that success. Could it be
that He meant for us to have more so we could help more
people besides ourselves? Hmm...

The problem with all this success and acquiring of
material possessions is that many are still left feeling empty,

wondering what is the true purpose of life and what is the good in the midst of all the getting. Because nothing that happens in our lives is an accident, we must conclude that God has a purpose for wealth and prosperity. He is the one who gives us the power to gain both of them. Notice I said both. That's because there is a difference between wealth and prosperity. One can be wealthy materially and yet be poor in spirit. On the other hand, one can be lacking in resources yet be prosperous because of a rich life well-lived. The mystery of finding the balance eludes many, though it doesn't have to.

There is an emptiness in living a fabulous life for just yourself. The fact is it's simply not fabulous. However, a life spent contributing to the needs of others out of the resources you have been blessed with leads to earthly blessings as well as those in heaven. A life of prosperity is available to all because you don't need a lot to live a rich life. If you have resources to give, that's wonderful, but the best gift you can give to others is yourself—your friendship, your ear to listen, your encouragement, your wisdom. Or, perhaps just the access to your home. Purposeful living is the richest life any of us can live, and yet the material world can distract us from all that we need to do to seek joy, peace, and a greater sense of accomplishment.

Lydia was a wealthy woman in Greek society with access to all the trappings a woman could want. Money, power, beautiful things, influential men, a packed social calendar, unlimited travel, and exciting experiences, yet she found all of these things insufficient to fulfill her completely. Her life gives us some profound, though they might seem unex-citing, principles for living a rich and powerful life. If we heed them, we, too, can have balanced lives filled with riches and power on every level.

Diva Principles

Lydia truly discovered the quiet basics and ran with them. What are the quiet basics? The first one is prayer. Her story reveals that she was a woman of prayer in the midst of a prayerless society. Believe me, the last thing anyone on her economic level was thinking about was prayer. Going to the Greek temple to worship the various gods that represented whatever they wanted was the order of the day. Anything it took to appease these voiceless, faceless wonders was rendered—from money to exorbitant gifts to prostitution. It was quite a scene. Lydia turned her back on all the deceptive hoopla to pursue a quiet life of prayer.

Prayer. Let's talk about this for a moment. There are several purposes for prayer. For most, the principle purpose is for getting God to do something we want Him to do, or for Him to give us something we want. That is not entirely what God had in mind. In His mind, prayer was for the purpose of nurturing intimacy with Him. Building a deep and passionate relationship. Out of that relationship would come all the trimmings we could possibly desire because that's what lovers do. They give gifts to the beloved. Some say they pray to center themselves. They're missing the point. There is nothing at our very center if God is not there. The fact is that prayer should center God in us. With Him firmly in place as the wheel in the middle of the wheel, as the axis at our core, things happen. Revelation happens that empowers us to acquire the desires of our heart, from inner peace to external success.

It is in that quiet place the still, small voice of God reveals secrets that set our heart, our mind, and our spirit free to do what we were created to do: Live out our purpose to its fullest. Oh, the sense of peace and fulfillment that can fill one when lying down at the end of the day, knowing that you accomplished all your purpose demanded for that day. A day that began in prayer.

Prayer and meditation is the prerequisite for victorious diva living. They are at the seat of power from which all sound decisions are made that fill one's life with all the soul longs for. In spite of Lydia's financial stature, accomplishments, and standing in the community, Lydia took the time to pray. Consistently and regularly. It was her lifeblood. She made the time for it. She had a place for it. And she did not swerve from this discipline. She met other women at a river to pray, seeking the face of God and His daily refreshing that enabled her to complete her demanding tasks. Lydia was devoted to God but longed to be instructed in His ways. After her conversion, God met with her, instructed her, and blessed her. The fruit of her interaction with Him was evident in her business. She excelled and was promoted through the combination of His spirit and her personal skills. She made God her business partner. Though she had everything materially, she still sought more. She sought God, knowing that what she truly craved could only be found in Him. She knew that great negotiation skills and social savvy were merely by-products of spending time in His presence where true wisdom was dispersed. So she went down to the river to pray without fail. Every day, three times a day and left others to wonder what was the secret of her success and the source of her serenity. Divas are prayer warriors. They know where their source of power and influence truly lies and plug into it.

Diva Confession

I will make God my divine partner personally and professionally. I will seek Him early and seek Him late, at all times I will seek Him. I will be passionate and disciplined in my pursuit of Him and all He has to offer me.

The second quiet basic is having a hunger for the truth of God's Word and the ability to live it out. Not just a craving, but an insatiable hunger. We are told that those who hunger after righteousness will be filled. Lydia longed to know more about God. She wanted to know His ways and what He expected of her. What exactly was her purpose? Why had she been given her specific giftings? God answered by sending Paul and the other disciples to teach her and her other lady friends. After hearing Paul's profound teaching, they longed to seal their covenant with God and were baptized.

Home improvement has become very popular in the last few years, but I find *self*-improvement at an all-time low. In spite of all the latest cosmetic innovations—teeth whitening, botox, liposuction, stomach stapling, tummy tucks, body sculpting, you name it, little attention is paid to the inside. Most self-help books are designed to get you what you want by teaching you how to influence others, but what about self-examination? How about taking responsibility for your own actions in order to bring about change in your world?

The greatest place we can all arrive at is the place of being able to admit we don't know quite as much as we think we do, because then we are ready to listen and learn. It was with hungry spirit that Lydia and the other women listened to Paul's teachings and thirsted to go deeper. In spite of all her material possessions, her spiritual life was her dearest asset and she nurtured it with a fervor.

It was through her interaction with God and learning of His ways that she discovered the true reason for her talents and success. For the good of others, her gifts were to be used, not privately hoarded in empty selfish living! Every diva knows that although she is successful, she is still first a child of God, second a woman, third someone who needs to give something of herself to others in order to be all she was created to be. In order to live a balanced life between career and a personal life, a woman must remain true to who she is, who she was designed to be. A life giver. A nurturer. This is where deep satisfaction will always be found because every woman's spirit craves to express itself in accordance with God's design.

Therefore, pursue a healthy spirit before a bulging bank account. Pursue peace above all the drama wheeling and dealing can bring. Follow after unity with God and social acceptance will find its right place in your life. Seek spiritual understanding and the knowledge you need will come into clear focus. Lydia prioritized her life in a way that made her fruitful in all her endeavors. As we recalibrate our spirits and align our minds with God's way of doing things, the power and success we seek will overwhelm us.

Diva Confession

I will make sure my spiritual foundation is firm before seeking to build my career or social standing. I will seek to balance my spiritual life with my professional life by being ever mindful of its purpose.

Lydia was baptized at the same river where she prayed and something became crystal clear as she emerged from the water. Everything she had was a gift from God, therefore she had to give something back! Her huge house was not just for her personal enjoyment. Her money was not to be hoarded, but given freely to a good cause that would further the purposes of God. So she urged Paul and the others to join her and her household and remain for as long as they needed to in order to complete their work. Her home became the first church in the area, open to all who were seeking help, healing, and truth. When Paul and Silas were miraculously released from jail, they returned to Lydia's house for safety and solace.

Though she was a dedicated Christian, Lydia was also able to deal effectively in the secular world. The success of her business suggests this. She excelled in her trade and had sound business relationships. She carried herself in such a manner that she became a beacon instead of a rock of offense. Many were drawn to God because of her witness. She managed her money well. Her needs were met with an abundance with more than enough left over to contribute to the needs of others.

At the end of the day, her ultimate fulfillment came from the things that were not tied to her career. The legacy she established came from the works she did beyond her business. It is important to remember that we work to live, not live to work. When we become consumed and ruled by our occupation, attempting to do it without God as our partner, work turns into labor. Hard, joyless, and unsatisfying. This was not God's design. He designed work to be another expression of His creative power through us, to benefit others. Another quiet basic.

Diva Confession

I will keep my work in perspective while seeking to use the resources I've been blessed with to benefit others. I will balance spirit with the reality of life and strive to be excellent in both.

Diva Do's and Don'ts

෫ Begin every day spending time alone with God. Keep Him as your premier business partner.

෫ Cultivate a life of prayer and consistent spiritual devotion.

෫ Search God's Word for wisdom. Proverbs is a great book for workable principles to live by in all areas of life.

෫ Surround yourself with other women of prayer and wisdom who can cover you and speak into your life in a beneficial way.

❧ Always be open to correction and direction.

❧ Take careful stock of your gifts and nurture them into a workable occupation.

❧ Have a profession—don't allow your profession to have you.

❧ Take care of business. Be excellent in all that you do and build a reputation for being consistent and reliable.

❧ Locate the needs of others that you are equipped to fill and reach out.

❧ Find creative ways to use your resources for sowing into the life of others.

Div-otion

You may say to yourself, "My power and the strength of my hands have produced this wealth for me." But remember the LORD your God, for it is he who gives you the ability to produce wealth... (Deuteronomy 8:17-18).

> *Dear heavenly Father, help me to keep You first in the midst of all that I strive to do and achieve. May I be ever mindful of Your voice and Your leading. And when the affairs of the world beckon too loudly, lead me back to the quiet place where I can hear You once again. Show me those who need the help that I can give and help me to give without reserve. Amen.*

The Shunammite Woman
(2 Kings 4:8-37; 8:1-6)

WHAT'S HER STORY:

She mastered the art of hospitality and giving of herself unconditionally. She never lost the faith in the face of what seemed to be a hopeless situation and learned an incredible lesson about restoration.

THE INSIDE SCOOP:

Though unnamed, this woman takes her place in the pages of biblical history because of her gift of hospitality. But beyond that, she had an unswerving faith in the face of tremendous challenge. After inviting a prophet of God, Elisha, to be a guest in her home and serving him with great care, Elisha perceives her desire for a child and blesses her to have one. However, the child dies a few years later. Undaunted by his death, this woman goes in pursuit of Elisha to come and raise her child from the dead, which he does! In later years under Elisha's direction, she leaves her home to avoid severe famine. After returning, she visits the king to retrieve her property. Upon hearing of her son's miraculous resurrection, he gives her back not only the land she once owned, but the profits of the land from the past seven years when she was absent!

POTENTIAL WEAKNESS:

She could have been so bitter about never having children that she would wallow in her own depression and self-pity, ignoring the opportunities around her for joy. After the death of her child, she could have concluded that God isn't really good after all and given up the fight to bring her son back to life. She could have gotten caught up in a blame game about all of her bad fortune.

STRENGTH:

She chose to live in the present and extend herself beyond her comfort zone. She never lost the faith and did not take the time to complain. She focused on the solution and pursued it.

DIVA-TUDE:

Her longing for the special faith that Elisha possessed made her tell her husband, "I know that this man who often comes our way is a holy man of God. Let's make a small room on the roof and put in it a bed and a table, a chair and a lamp for him. Then he can stay there whenever he comes to us."

THE TOUCH THAT MADE THE DIFFERENCE:

Her no-nonsense approach to life caused her to truly appreciate the prophet Elisha and his forthright approach to faith in God. She took pleasure in extending the gift of hospitality to him, never dreaming of the reward that she would reap for doing so.

The Persona
of a Diva

Some people always manage to look good on paper despite what is going on beneath the surface. This is a truly divine quality to possess. "Never let them see you sweat." I think the philosophy goes deeper than that—to having immovable faith no matter what is happening around you. It is called the approach to life. Do you see the glass as half-empty or half-full? What do you do when life hands you a bowl of lemons? Suck in your cheeks or make lemonade? Do you know how to transfer pain into a positive thing? Or are you bowed by it? Have you mastered the art of living *over* your circumstances? Have you learned to transfer your longings into giving?

Hmm...so many questions, so little time, and yet these are very real and very important parts of your attitude that must be addressed. They affect your ability to find yourself in the right place for just the blessing you have been longing for. Receiving the desires of your heart is extremely reliant on how open you are to blessing others and giving of yourself. It is more blessed to give than to receive because giving always guarantees you a return greater than you expected, while simply receiving ends the moment the action has been rendered.

Like a stone rolling down the side of a hill, it gathers speed as it goes because it is in motion. Stagnation leads to just that, further stagnation. The momentum of living and giving will always attract things beyond your wildest dreams. The greatest storehouse a woman possesses is her home, if it is filled with the right things. Warmth, encouragement, loving attention, sensitivity to others, a servant's heart, and a hospitable spirit. The aroma of these things will always bring others to your door. As they receive blessings from you, they are sure to bless you back.

Everyone, for the most part, wants to know they have value, they are cared for, and they matter. When we open our doors to people, all of the above are confirmed in their hearts and minds. When others matter enough to you for you to invest time and energy in making them feel welcome and full, they cannot walk away without contemplating what gift they could render to you for creating such a good feeling within them. Ah…but the attitude has everything to do with the act. Are you able to serve others without seeking anything in return becomes the big question. Can you do all in your power to bless someone just because?

I love to watch people eat my food. They love to eat it. And I love to watch. That is my satisfaction. They don't have to say a word, the smile on their face says it all. I try to capture that image as often as possible by finding every excuse to invite someone over for dinner. They feel special because I took the time to prepare something especially for them. Good feelings and conversation are always shared over the dinner table. Inevitably, in the middle of the following week

I receive a present, a call to say how much it was appreciated, an invitation—their treat to repay me for a wonderful evening. My circle of friends is large because of this tradition, but dare I say I have never had a reluctant guest. And when I'm feeling my most down, I strive to turn my attention outward and see who I can impart a good feeling to because I know that good feelings will be returned.

The Shunammite woman looked good on paper. Wealthy, prominent, influential in her social circle, blessed with a generous husband and yet she had her own secret longings yet to be fulfilled, but it did not deter her from using the gift she already had—the gift of hospitality. Let's take a look at why cultivating this facet of your womanhood is so important by gleaning from the principles her story reveals.

Diva Principles

First, one should know who to invite to their home! The Shunammite woman recognized something special about Elisha and submitted her thought to her husband. This was a man of God, he was not like the other preachers who had come to town. There was something different about him. Someone she felt she should invest in by making herself available to his service. She didn't just do what was convenient to serve him, she went the extra mile! She had a room built for him on the roof of her house.

Truly serving someone is, for the most part, inconvenient. Decisions must be made: How important is this person to you? What is their value in your life? How will you show them their worth to you? Consider the fact even cooking a meal versus ordering in or going out to dinner can be inconvenient given anyone's crammed schedule in today's world. This simple act of investing in someone can leave deep, life-changing impressions with them as well as yourself.

This woman decides to build Elisha his own room and to furnish it with a bed, table, chair, and lamp stand. She wanted him to have a place to rest, to be fed, and also have light. This should be our desire for those we care for as well as those God assigns to us to nurture. We must be able to perceive the heart and spirits of those around us and know when it is time to invest in them.

Do you offer rest, sustenance, and light to those in your world or are you too busy? Caught up in the rat race of life ignoring all the signals that this one person might be the key to discovering something greater in you? To birthing something your heart has harbored for a long time? It might be something as simple as a quiet conversation, or as amazing as a fabulous gift. Remember, whatever you reap, you must sow first.

Whenever Elisha passed through town, he resided in this special room that was prepared just for him. One day he could no longer stand just receiving and decided it was time to bless her. Now that's key. You can't time a blessing in your life but give anyway. People will rarely give you what you think they should or at the time you think they should. Around the time that you are no longer looking, you receive what I call a kiss from heaven. A reminder that God will not allow your kindness to be forgotten if you give from a self-less heart.

When Elisha asked what he could do for her, this woman merely says, "I am content." She had learned to accept the cards that had been dealt to her and play them. However, the one that she had blessed was not content with that answer. And truly, hearts you have touched will not rest until they are able to touch you back in a way that matters significantly. Just as she had sought to fill what was missing in his life, he now returned the favor by noting the absence of a child in her life. So he chose to bless her and God cooperated and granted her a child.

Like those who are childless, waiting to conceive year after year, then deciding to adopt only to find themselves pregnant shortly thereafter, the economy of God is simply this: What you make room for will come to you. Every diva enlarges the door of her heart and home to accommodate greater blessings than presently exist in her world.

Hospitality is a gift (it costs you nothing to offer), yet the returns are endless. Learning to make your house a home that is considered a respite for others will fill you to overflowing in ways you could never imagine.

Diva Confession

I will purpose to offer to others what I long for myself. I will constantly seek to give selflessly anticipating God's remembrance of where I reside. I will live in the moment and find present joy in the day-to-day of reaching out to others.

Unfortunately, the gift she was given, this child who was her greatest joy, also caused her to experience her greatest pain. The child died. However, she didn't miss a beat. Quietly placing him on the prophet's bed, she went off in search of Elisha to remedy the problem. She did not grieve, ask "why me?" or even hesitate about what her next step was to be. Divas do not give in easily to crisis. They do not allow it to change their demeanor. They understand disappointments and setbacks are inevitable, but misery is optional.

She did not call friends to broadcast her woe. She did not transfer her pain to her husband. She made the quiet decision to pursue a solution before getting everyone excited. If all else failed, she would then resign herself to her loss and weather it by continuing her life gracefully, treasuring the moments when she had a son, being thankful for that time.

There is a tree that grows on the mountainside in Lebanon that has been cruelly broken by the strong winds that rage against the side of these enormous hills time and time again. In their brokenness, they grow anyway, releasing resin to patch the break. They grow tall in spite of the elements that threaten to destroy them. Over time, the cedars of Lebanon gained the reputation for being the strongest of woods. They were the first choice for building King Solomon's palace as well as the supports for the temple in Jerusalem. Those who weather the storms of life and stand the test of time and tribulation eventually receive the honor due them.

Trouble is the refiner of integrity and character. It births a graciousness if allowed to do so. A diva becomes truly divine when she bows under the weight of her pain and then rises from the ashes, smoothing her garments to continue on her way. Never breaking, always bending and lifting herself to a place higher than she was before.

How is this possible you ask? Because her faith is not in herself or even what she sees. She has placed her trust in a higher place, in One who is supreme. She realizes God allows hard times to come and makes the decision to endure them by keeping her eyes fixed squarely on Him for the deliverance of all that she needs or desires. She says in the face of trial, "This is just a test." One that she will pass with flying colors.

It was with this attitude that the Shunammite went in search of the one who had blessed her to see if he would bless her again. When asked if all was well with her, her husband, and her child she answered quietly, "All is well." Because she chose to believe it would be.

What can I say about this woman? The enormity of what transpired is overwhelming. She opens her home to someone who then gives her something that causes her pain. A pain that surpasses any pain that she has ever experienced before. And yet she goes to him. She does not draw up in bitterness thinking to herself, "So this is the thanks I get!" No, she faces the issue head on and demands an acceptable solution. "As sure as the Lord lives and you live I will not return without you!" (2 Kings 4:30 NBV). In short, "I am holding you accountable and expect you to responsibly respond to my loss and do something."

This is big! The courage to face your pain and believe in an answer involves your entire will. She never lost her composure and because of what her persona demanded, he went with her. She left him with the child and waited patiently until the boy had been resurrected. When called to receive her son back into her arms, she first bowed herself to the ground at the feet of Elisha in gratitude before reaching for the greatest love of her life.

The blame game does not a gracious person make, but giving others the opportunity to play a part in blessing your life does. To be able to state a need and walk away leaving the other to search their own resourcefulness for an answer is a gift to that person. They will go the extra mile for you. Severing her friendship with Elisha would not have gotten her what she wanted, but seeking his help and assistance in restitution made the bond of their friendship even closer. It was with humility and sincere gratitude that she bowed at his feet before reaching for what she really wanted to hold the moment she entered the room. Divas always acknowledge the source of their blessing. Whether it be to people or God, they render honor—shamelessly understanding that humility is supreme.

Diva Confession

*I will not be bowed by bitterness but will
arise with grace to embrace even those
that I see as the source of my pain.
I will give honor where it is due and will
not harbor blame. I will stand in the face
of trial and disappointment keeping
my eyes on the true source of strength and
restoration. I will embrace it with no
thought of past challenges.*

Not only was the life of her son restored, but a deeper relationship with Elisha and a greater belief in the power of God was cemented in her spirit. Elisha had proven his faithfulness as a friend to her. As one who was willing to intercede on her behalf to a God who loved her and willingly responded. So when Elisha advised her to go to the land of the Philistines to avoid famine she went with no questions, knowing his counsel had passed the test of reliability in her life. She could now walk away from all she possessed without a backward glance because she had already experienced loss and restoration. She could trust God to keep her land safe and return it at the right time. And so she went. Seven years later she returned. With bold confidence, she stood before the king and asked for the return of her land. Once again God honored her unmovable faith and gave her back more than she asked for.

It is true we get what we expect. Our expectations affect our countenance and our posture and signal to others if they should take our request seriously or not. Divas walk in constant expectation of blessing, promotion, and open doors. They keep their eyes fixed on an open heaven. Not out of a sense of entitlement, but from a heart that believes God wants to bless them. Because they are cognizant of His heart and His will for their lives, the things they desire are not fanciful, but real and reasonable to God. They are founded on what He has promised and because God agrees, He answers. Now I must attest to the indulgence of God at this point, and tell you that He does like to pamper His women, so stretch your faith a bit to include some of the trimmings you wouldn't ordinarily expect.

It's safe to say those who know who they are and who they serve are able to walk in the expectation of their desires being fulfilled. I recall being in Beverly Hills several years ago, driving past one of their hottest restaurants. On the spur of the moment I said to my friends, "Ooh! Let's have lunch there!" To which my friends responded, "Girl, you have to have reservations to get in there, and you have to call a week in advance to get a spot." To which I said, "We'll see about that. Just follow me and let me handle this." On that note, we pulled up to the valet and entered the restaurant. I went up to the host and announced myself. "McKinney Hammond for 3." He said, "One moment." He scanned his book for my reservation, (of course he saw none) as I stood smiling and waiting. He scanned it again, then took three menus under his arm and said, "Right this way!" We were seated next to someone very famous and had a fabulous lunch. After we sat down, my friends doubled over in laughter and just lost it. After recovering, they looked at me and said, "How on earth do you always do these things and get away with it?" I leaned forward and said with my best diva face and accent, "Dahling, one merely needs to look the part and behave as though they belong where they are. In the face of such confidence who would question them?" My girlfriends conceded that this was a valuable lesson to learn and one that could be applied across the board in life.

In spite of loss or disappointment, divas know their true worth and do not shrink from seeking it. They do not second-guess God or themselves because they have a proven track record of His goodness. They have a determination to survive and excel against all odds. Like the cedar she bows but does not break, releasing what she needs to in order to heal herself, enduring the test of time and stormy weather. No matter what you have endured, the parting comment that should be echoed behind you when you leave a room is, "There goes a great woman."

Diva Confession

*I will learn to wear life and all I hold dear
loosely, entrusting it into God's care. I will
accept losses as gracefully as I accept
blessings, always believing in the power of
God to restore what is rightfully mine.
I will be cognizant of my worth in God's
sight as well as His desire to bless me. I will
walk in expectancy of my heart's
desires being met.*

Diva Do's and Don'ts

❧ Choose to deliberately live outside of yourself by reaching out to others.

❧ Seek ways to invest in the lives of those you perceive as special assignments from God to you.

❧ Be willing to stretch beyond your comfort zone of convenience for someone.

❧ Purpose to make your home a haven. Find ways to make every guest experience rest, nourishment, and light.

❧ Receive gifts gracefully but never expect them.

❧ When disappointment comes, walk softly and resist the urge to submerge yourself in your pain. Focus on finding a solution.

- Do not stir up negativity around you or spread it to other loved ones, try to diffuse issues before they reach impasse.

- In the face of a trial, allow others to rise to the occasion for you.

- Exercise humility and a grateful heart with those who come to your aid.

- Do not cast blame. See if you are part of the problem.

- Never give up.

- Embrace and use pain to make you stronger. Allow it to finish its work in you until grace envelops your character.

- Purpose to live life gracefully at all costs.

- At all times trust God.

Div-otion

Consider it pure joy, my brothers, [my sisters] whenever you face trials of many kinds, because you know that the testing of your faith develops perseverance. Perseverance must finish its work so that you may be mature and complete, not lacking anything (James 1:2-4).

> *Dear heavenly Father, help me to learn to live life gracefully. As I grow through the giving of myself and weathering life's difficulties, instill within me sound character and integrity that bring glory to you and blessing to others. Amen.*

Get Your Act Together, Woman!

Diva Profile

The Proverbs 31 Woman
(Proverbs 31:10-31)

WHAT'S HER STORY:

This woman mastered the art of being a complete diva and solidifed her place in history as the woman who surpasses all others because of her virtues.

THE INSIDE SCOOP:

Long heralded as the ultimate woman that every man should aspire to find. Her long list of incredible achievements have left many a woman in awe. Here was a woman who could bring home the bacon, fry it up in a pan, make her man feel like a man, raise children who would be a credit to their name, keep her household running smoothly, be a successful entrepreneur, and still have time for charity work. Whew! Now that's a divine diva.

POTENTIAL WEAKNESS:

She could have become overwhelmed by her list of responsibilities. She could have been distracted by selfish ambition and misplaced her priorities to the detriment of her family and others who would have profited from her presence and input.

STRENGTH:

She understood the seasons of her life and her value to her household. She also had a full understanding of her purpose—she embraced it, celebrated it, and took one day at a time. She remained fully present in every circumstance she found herself in, never wandering ahead, lagging behind, or determining that the grass was greener on the other side.

DIVA-TUDE:

The writer of the book says it best, "She openeth her mouth with wisdom and the law of kindness is on her tongue" (Proverbs 31:26 ASV).

THE TOUCH THAT MADE THE DIFFERENCE:

Her strong belief in God gave her the assurance her life mattered and her contributions would make a positive difference in the lives of all she encountered. As she strove to be a woman approved of by God, her virtues were noted by everyone in her life and she was given credit where it was due.

The Composite of a Diva

What exactly does a diva look like? Her description could surprise you. I would dare to say you've met many of them, unaware you had an encounter with a consummate woman. She wasn't swathed in fur and sequins. She didn't talk with an accent or have an affected walk. She might not have been glamorous at all. As a matter of fact, quite the opposite. But there was something about her. You didn't know what it was but she was... different.

More than likely she was gracefully wearing her life along with her unassuming attire. Just being herself without seeking any credit. Never boasting about her list of wonderful attributes that you'd never know until you got into a lengthy discussion with her, discovering surprising things about this woman who wore no flag. Things like how she gave up a flourishing career to stay at home with her children for years, or how she started an incredible business from scratch that is now soaring in profits while benefiting many. Or, how she encouraged her husband to leave his safe job and pursue his dreams. How she partnered with him to help him become the success he is today.

And then there is her amazing gift of hospitality. How she single-handedly decorated their incredible house. How she made the scrumptious meal you just knew had to be ordered in. How she balances being famous and gracious at the same time in spite of a harrowing schedule. How she left a plush life to answer the call of God to live among and serve the poor. The list could go on and on to describe all these different women who do it all or one trait at a time. The bottom line is they just do what they do by the grace of God.

What does this woman look like? Is she tall, short, slender, stocky, redhead or blonde? Blue-eyed or intensely dark brown? There is no set external description because this woman is comfortable with herself whatever size, color, or manner of dress. The thing that sets her apart and makes her distinct from the rest is the composite of her character. Her internal qualities continually transform her outer appearance and give her regal bearing—even when she's clothed in sweats or jeans. Whether hauling laundry or standing at the helm of a powerful conglomerate, she is a lady. Graceful and gracious, doing what she does in excellence without despising her femininity. She is in fact, a Proverbs 31 woman.

Perhaps that is why I choose not to be intimidated by this mother's description of what her son should look for in a woman. I understand all these exploits weren't done in a day, but in measured seasons and increments as she came slowly into the complete understanding of her purpose as a woman.

Let's cross the final frontier of this divine study by gleaning principles from the one woman who embodies all that we have considered thus far and more. Let her confirm the answer to this resounding thought: *Is it possible to be a diva?* Most definitely!

Diva Principles

There are several layers to the Proverbs 31 woman I think we need to peel back one by one, like personality, habits, and results. On the other hand, we also need to consider how she took care of herself, her household, and others because these contributed to the results and response she received from others.

Throughout the book of Proverbs, warnings are given about avoiding the wrong type of women—strange, bold, promiscuous women who could not be trusted. Small wonder the first qualification for being a Proverbs 31 woman is trustworthiness. She is a woman of uncompromising character—faithful, loyal, and sound. Because she is a woman who fears the Lord and respects His commands, she conducts herself in a fashion that is above reproach. Not because of *man* but because she walks in submission to a Power greater than herself. She respects the handiwork of God by treating the people He created with respect and honesty. From her servants to the merchants she traded with, to her own children and husband, each was treated with kindness, humility, and grace. Every person she interacted with on a daily basis was liberated to feel as if they were important to her no matter how great or small their contributions. She listened to them, responded to their individual needs, and kept their secrets. She was a kind and nonjudgmental confidante. One who could be relied upon in time of need or crisis. A friend, a sister, and a faithful lover. This was the foundation of who she was and where all divine divas must begin....Always bearing the best of intentions toward those in their world.

There was no repeating of matters that can separate friends in this woman's spirit. No manipulative criticisms, or withholding of due praise and encouragement. No, this was a woman who was comfortable in the skin she was in, free to allow others to feel the same. Her countenance and character provided a respite for those weary from being on guard and gave rest to those who needed the heart of a friend who would simply allow them to be who they were without thought or pretense.

Diva Confession

I will walk in a trustworthy fashion at all times with those in my personal world as well as those at-large in my community. I will seek to be a haven to those who find it hard to be at rest.

Career Savvy

Oh, but that is just the beginning! This was a strong woman, a willing worker. Now let's back up here. She neither considered work to be beneath her nor did it begrudgingly. She threw herself into it with passion and chose to revel in productivity. Diligent, rising early, and going to bed late, she mastered the art of following through and completing her mission. One can only have passion for her work if she is pursuing things in the area of her natural gifting. Many people go to work every day counting the minutes to closing because they hate their job. Excellence goes out the window, replaced by mediocrity and low productivity. On the flip side, consider the musician who loses track of time so lost is she in the working of her craft. Whatever your job is, make sure it is something you love to do. Passion is everything when it comes to one's profession; it makes the difference between thriving and surviving to get a paycheck. All of this woman's senses were involved with the things she chose to tackle that reaped her profit. She not only gained financial dividends but immense pleasure from the tasks she did. She was able to stand back and make intelligent assessments about her ventures. She could see her merchandise was good and know its true value when she entered the marketplace to trade.

Not a bone of insecurity was in her body, she knew what she had to offer and was able to command the right price. Obviously others were convinced and willing to pay. She was able to discern what was needed in the marketplace and created her niche from that place of need. She was creative in choosing work that ranged from traditional to nontraditional for her day, and was not questioned because she worked and walked in excellence. From making clothes to real estate investments, to farming and merchandising, she took a little and worked it until it increased and produced a rich harvest. A diva knows she is not defined by her work but by the quality of it. She carefully chooses from among her natural gifts and develops them into a productive craft that will bless others and bring her personal joy and satisfaction. She knows to work is one thing, but to work out your passion in excellence is truly divine.

Diva Confession

*I will consider my gifts and use them to
bless others, knowing if that is my
motivation I will naturally prosper. I will
seek to work in the area of my passion
and perform in excellence.*

Mastering Organization

In order to be successful in any area, you must exercise wisdom and plan carefully. If wisdom will bring you wealth, happiness, honor, and long life, then careful planning will *surely* help you secure it. Today, many women are overwhelmed with juggling their household duties with the demands of a career...throw in a family and it's all up for grabs! I am a huge fan of journals, calendars, diaries, and writing things down. Of putting systems in place that ensure sidestepping needless emergencies, dramas, overload, and burnout. Often things are allowed to pile up until they reach unmanageable proportions. This woman did not worry about the future because she responsibly anticipated and prepared for it. She was not behind the eight ball but in front of it, one step ahead of the game.

I am still amazed at all the things my mother accomplished when I was a child. She worked a nine-to-five administrative job, yet still managed to have a hot meal on the table everyday, including fresh homecooked baked goods and desserts I might add. On top of this, she ruled a spotless home, sewed clothing for the entire household, managed to look flawless, and go to bed at a reasonable time. How did she do all of this? I would see her sitting at the kitchen table with her notebook, planning her work and later working her plan. She had a system. And it did not include being superwoman. She mapped out the goals for the week and enlisted everyone in the household to fulfill various tasks. Together, the house ran like a smooth unit. She would write out her menu for the week, then make her grocery list. On the appointed day, my father had the job of buying the groceries. This was the deal because if my mother was cut loose in the grocery store to sample new and interesting delights, we would go over budget, whereas my dad would just stick to the list.

This being done, it was my job to put the groceries away. Saturday was cooking and baking day. Ooh...the smells that would come from that kitchen! When she got to the bread and the cinnamon-topped rolls, it was as if an alarm sounded in the neighborhood. People would line up for one of her famous scrumptious rolls of which she always made extra for just this purpose. Meal after meal was assembled and frozen. The menu was placed on the refrigerator door along with instructions. It was the job of whoever got home first to take the defrosted meal out of the refrigerator, place it in the oven, prepare the vegetables or salad that was to accompany it, and set the table. At exactly 6:30 P.M., everyone sat down to eat. The children washed the dishes, finished any leftover homework, and were in bed by 10 P.M. on the dot—no sooner, no later.

Meanwhile, for her own entertainment, my mother would sew outfits for the family and herself. Later, as I entered junior high, she taught me to make my own clothing. Saturday evening was beautifying time. Yes, my mother could even wield a mean curling iron. She had done hair to supplement her income while in college. Sunday was a day of rest. And then the week began again like clockwork. As we got older, my father developed a love of cooking and the cooking duties became shared ones. She went on to become entrepreneurial in her own right, later leaving her job for a profitable career as a Mary Kay director. She returned to her first love, making people beautiful.

Today, as I shake my head in amazement at all she did when I was growing up, she shakes her head along with me and admits she doesn't know how she did it herself. In her eyes, she was on automatic, simply doing what she had to do. I can see the bigger picture in retrospect. She was a woman with a plan and she knew how to work it. For more help with putting a plan into action in your own life I recommend consulting a Web site or book designed to help you do just that. Log on to flylady.net for help with personalizing a plan that will make you more effective.

Organization is everything and admitting you are not superwoman is just as important. Never be ashamed to ask for help. Enlisting everyone is not just making your load lighter, but teaching others to be responsible citizens as well. Chores build character in children and give them an appreciation for work that will benefit them in the years to come. They will truly understand what life costs and be prepared for the real world. It also allows others to share in your labor. To feel as if they are making a valuable contribution to the household. It gives them a sense of ownership and investment in their home as well as a partnership with their parents. This kills the temptation for teenagers to behave as if they are staying at a hotel where they are not expected to make any contributions, or be personally responsible for their own space or that of others. It causes each family member to care about creating an environment everyone enjoys dwelling in.

What are some simple steps you can take to gain control out of a home that has taken on a life of its own and still lead a balanced existence? Consider these tips:

❧ Make a list of all your household duties and weekly errands.

❧ Allocate how much time you feel each task will take to be completed. This way you can get rid of the smaller tasks first.

❧ Prioritize their order of importance and then assign each major task to a different day. Perhaps Monday evening is when you do your dusting, Tuesday your laundry, etc.

❧ Enlist the help of your family. Find out what people's favorite tasks are and assign accordingly. Rotate them from time to time so everyone is well-rounded in experience. If you live alone, take one day at a time and try to stick to your schedule. Don't beat yourself up if you don't. Persist until it becomes a habit to you. Don't be too prideful to ask for help. God created us to depend on one another, you will be surprised how happy a sibling, friend, or neighbor may be to help you.

❧ If you can afford help, as in a cleaning lady, by all means go for it. Here is where that change jar could come in handy again. Perhaps they only come every two weeks or once a month to do major cleaning chores, leaving you with only the maintenance work. Every little bit helps. You would be amazed at how reasonable some maid services are. Depending on the space you have and what you want done, you can pay anywhere from $45 and up. Most services are bonded and as you continue to use the same person over time, you find you have a trusted worker who will go the extra mile for you. Many years ago, I broke down and made the budget sacrifice to get help. I enlisted the wife of the janitor in my apartment building. She has been with me for more than seven years. When I informed her I had bought a home and was moving, she wept. She now drives across town to help me. She has become a mother to me and treats my home and possessions with the same loving concern as if they were her own. If she notices something needs fixing, she enlists her husband to fix it and tells me about it later! At first I felt ashamed that I was not able to be on top of maintaining my home. I felt like a failure but wise friends counseled me to consider my priorities. As I entered into full time ministry, it became a matter of where my time was best spent. After all, mopping and polishing my floor would seriously take away from me finishing this book or preparing a message for women who need help and inspiration!

❦ Be honest about your limitations and prioritize.

❦ Build rest time into your calendar along with your duties to keep your life in balance. Rome was not built in a day.

Diva Confession

*I will assess my duties and responsibilities,
prioritize, and realistically set goals
for myself. I will rejoice in the fact I am not
superwoman and will empower others
by seeking their assistance. I will purpose to
live a balanced life in spite of my
many obligations.*

Dealing with Finances

When you are juggling a lot of hats, it is imperative that you be resourceful and financially responsible. This detail cannot be overlooked because it can cause a major fire in the engine of a fine-tuned machine if you run out of financial fuel, causing great instability, needless mental stress, and aggravation. One of the biggest stresses in life is finances, in a marriage or as a single, as people fight to keep all their financial balls in the air at the same time. We've discussed shopping earlier, but now let's run the rest of the gamut from the basics, such as household goods, to longer-term investments. This woman was on top of her money from her groceries to purchasing land and turning it over for a profit.

Money scares many of us so we avoid the topic like the plague. I have been guilty of this for years myself. Never understood it, didn't want to deal with it, and my father was a banker! Even if you ignore it, it doesn't go away. As a matter of fact, if you ignore money matters, debt will pile up. Make decisions concerning how you need to budget, spend your money and stick to the budget no matter what temptation brings your way. Recreational shopping may be a stress-buster but it can bust more than that—it can bust your wallet. I have a friend who is so disciplined in this area. When invited to go shopping she simply says, "Nope, I am not purchasing anything that is not on my list of present needs right now." In the face of, "Well we can just go to look?" She strongly replies, "What is the point!?" Here is a woman who knows her limitations. She has a plan and she sticks to it.

I am no Suze Orman or Larry Burkett, therefore I strongly recommend getting their books on how to handle your finances. In the meantime, for those who are still a little shy on the subject, I would like to make a few suggestions.

- First, God asks for a ten percent tithe of your income. This is the first bill I pay because if it weren't for Him, I wouldn't have anything. Uncle Sam asks for more than God does, so this should not be a hardship on your attitude. Uncle Sam fixes your roads and protects the land, but God gives you the breath you breathe, as well as the ability to do your job and make a living.

- Secondly, tithe to yourself. Put ten percent in a savings account and purpose not to touch it. If you can stretch open another expendable savings, put another ten percent there. The goal is to have a nest egg of six months to a year of your monthly budget in case you find yourself out of work or unable to work. God does not want us to live a life of panic, running frantically to put out fires instead of being able to calmly assess our situation and move forward without fear.

- When buying anything from groceries to clothing to household items, furniture and even automobiles, do your homework and shop for a good deal. Know your market and don't pay more than you have to out of impatience. Check with others who are versed on the subject of what you are looking for. Rumor has it you should take a man with you when shopping for a car, to ensure you are not being taken advantage of. It is assumed that women are easy marks on a car lot. Many advise that you should never buy a brand-new car because it depreciates at least 20 percent the minute you drive it off the lot and goes down from there. Some cars depreciate faster than others, some trade and resale better. Know the inside scoop before you buy.

✑ Look for savings and clip coupons. Rich people have money because they don't spend it at random. They are the most cost-conscious people you will meet. They rarely pay full price for anything unless it is something that they know will appreciate in value.

✑ Invest in real estate. Buy a home, a condo, something! There are so many programs available now for purchasing with no money down that one is without excuse. As a single woman, it took me a long time to get this one. Think about it this way for those who shiver at the responsibility. The difference between owning and renting is the same as the difference between living together and being married—commitment with a greater return. When you own the place where you are living, you are building financial security for yourself. Don't buy at random, investigate the neighborhood and assess its future value. Not only will you find that you feel better about paying a mortgage versus rent because it's yours, you will definitely have a sense of empowerment because you own something.

✑ Consult with a personal banker to find out about savings plans and options at your bank that yield higher interest than you are presently getting on your regular savings account. If your job has not instituted an IRA or 401K account for you, make sure you do it yourself.

✑ Make an allowance for your guilty pleasures and indulgences. Allocate how many of them you can afford a year and link them to a special occasion so you don't get out of control.

༉ Decide to take control of your finances and do some plastic surgery. Yes, that's right—cut up all those credit cards and try to keep just one for emergencies, travel, etc. Do not purchase more than you can pay for when the statement comes. Never pay just the minimum. Always pay more. If possible, pay the full balance to avoid interest. What you saved on a sale you will pay in interest if you allow it to run amuck. Pay on time! Your credit rating is vitally important. It can haunt you for years to come and hinder you when you least expect it.

༉ Seek a financial counselor if you have no idea how to budget or save, they are usually quite creative with setting up a structure you can follow. Another helpful resource for financial advice is cheapskatemonthly.com. You can log on to the Web site for free advice or subscribe for more in-depth assistance.

༉ Separate your needs from your wants. Be honest with yourself and make responsible decisions. When being undisciplined, ask the Holy Spirit to put you in check when making unwise purchases. Be sensitive to His leading and obedient when He waves the red flag. Consider the fact that God has entrusted you with the money you have. How would you like someone to care for the money you gave them to keep for you? Choose to be responsible with what you are given so that He can trust you with more.

Diva Confession

I will become the master of my money.
I will not be ruled by impulse but will make
wise and discerning choices concerning
my finances. I will partner with God to
create security for my future by
watching how I spend today.

Making Your House a Home

Every woman is under tremendous pressure as the world makes more and more demands on us to be productive. Yet we must take time to delight in the small things and have a harbor—a safe haven to retreat to for refreshment and restoration. Though the Proverbs 31 woman was a hard worker, she still had an eye for the finer things and cultivated that area of her life. She sought to make her home beautiful. She selected rich tapestries for drapes and made quilted coverings for her bed. I'm sure her home was filled with fresh flowers gathered after a day of farming or a day at the market. She made her house a home. She cultivated good taste in her household. She paid attention to the details and filled the house with her touch.

This is where a woman gets to shine and revel in all her feminine gifts. This is your domain if you decide to claim it. You may run a company, but still be at the beck and call of others. But your home, well, it's completely yours. Decorate it with all of your favorite creative impulses. I don't know about you, but I am addicted to the home decorating channels. It's amazing the things that you can do, without paying a small ransom, to add life to a room. How colors and textures play a large part in setting the atmosphere and mood in a room.

Home decorating has become the national pastime in the last few years. With the rise of incredible stores rich with resources for doing-it-yourself, everyone is busy measuring and hammering away. Midnight jaunts to Home Depot can get you in just as much trouble as your favorite clothing store once you get the decorating fever! Places like Pottery Barn, Expo, Hobby Lobby, The Great Indoors, Z Gallery, Restoration Hardware, Crate and Barrel, The Container Store...oh, shall I go on? All of these wonderful stores offer everything a woman needs to become the queen of her personal castle in style. Never overlook antique shops and fairs as well as higher-end, second-hand shops where you can find priceless pieces that can be refinished. Pillows and candles can be an inexpensive touch that add an extra spark and sets the atmosphere for relaxation and comfort. Indulge in the little things that make a big difference in your home.

A diva knows how to make a statement without talking. She is able to express who she is and how she feels about others by the atmosphere she perpetuates in her home. She sets the stage for comfort and security by decorating her home as well as her own spirit with beautiful things that draw others to the center of her world. Domesticity is not viewed as something that is beneath her but rather some-thing to be mastered and personalized to her specific design. It is an avenue of creative expression as well as a revelation of her spirit to those who visit or remain.

Diva Confession

I will master the art of making a house a home. I will seek to create an atmosphere and setting that is an oasis for my family and friends. I will take thoughtful care and attention to the details of my surroundings that will not only reflect my heart for those I love, but also provide comfort and nourishment for those who spend time in my home.

Diva-licious Cooking & Meal Planning

Speaking of making a house a home, it is now time to tackle a crucial subject: cooking. A lost art to many women these days but nonetheless important. The saying, "The way to a man's heart is through his stomach," didn't just pop into someone's mind one day. It is true. But not just a man's heart, *anyone's* heart is touched when someone takes the time to prepare a meal and serve it to them. You are actually imparting a portion of yourself when you cook a meal and serve it to someone. There's a spiritual component to it.

Food represents more than just a regular meal. It represents love, security, care, and even comfort to the ones that you serve. The most intimate of details are shared over food. Sharing a meal is communion. It is literally touching the person you are eating with in a way that bridges the pathway of communication. Years ago, when families ate together regularly, they were much more in touch with what was going on with one another. Problems were revealed and solved at the dinner table. Now we're so caught up in the day-to-day, most families are having long-distance relationships although they live in the same house! Sometimes it takes a tragedy to get people back in touch with one another. This is not how God intended the family unit to function. The dinner table was to be a time of sharing and exchanging. Of encouraging and lifting one another up to have the strength and wisdom to carry out the day-to-day art of living life well, together and individually. Jesus was a stickler for breaking bread with His disciples, His core inner group, as well as with others He was reaching out to. Some of their deepest conversations took place while partaking of a meal. Small wonder a meal was especially significant to Him the night before His betrayal where He shared His last bits of wisdom with those closest to Himself. The dinner table should be like a watering hole where the members of one body gather for daily refreshing.

Even single women should master the art of cooking and learn to do it well. Practice makes perfect. Now is the time to experiment on dishes and build a nice repertoire. Invite friends over and learn how to serve, how to make a table beautiful, and how to nurture good, quality conversation.

I find that most women who do not like to cook, don't like to because they don't know how. It is an overwhelming chore to them instead of something that brings them joy. This is an easy problem to solve. My mentor, P.B. Wilson, will confess that for years she avoided her kitchen. But when she got the revelation on the power of cooking, she determined to become a great cook. Her solution was simple. Whenever she tasted something she liked, she would ask the person who prepared it to show her how they had made it. She took copious notes and then cooked it herself. To her amazement, not only did she become quite a chef in her own right, she found herself enjoying preparing dishes to serve to those she loved. It became a bridge to her mentoring other women on the art of homemaking. It has revolutionized countless marriages and empowered women to take over an area of their homes they dreaded approaching.

The Bible says the Proverbs 31 woman was like a merchant ship bringing her food from afar. That translates in my eyes to variety. Merchant ships stopped at different ports and collected the most exotic of fare to bring to their final destination. Today's woman not only has access to farmers markets with tons of fresh produce, but also to a variety of stores that offer all you can imagine when it comes to the most basic of staples and any assortment of treats from around the world. The possibilities are endless when it comes to choices for eating well. You don't have to be a major gourmet chef, simple good food will suffice. Learning how to garnish plates to make things look delectable is right up our alley because we were born to be creative. The bottom line is learn the basics and be creative. From grocery stores to more specialized shops like Whole Foods or Trader Joe's that offer more natural and organic sorts of things, the possibilities are endless.

Let's not forget the Sam's Clubs and Costcos of the world where you can buy goods in bulk and save a ton of money! There is no excuse not to be able to prepare the most basic of dishes. Why, many of these places have already prepared and seasoned the meats and dishes so that all you have to do is heat them up! I highly recommend making things from scratch as much as possible so you can control the level of sodium and sugar in your diet.

So if you are one who is afraid of the kitchen, take a deep breath...you can do this. I am going to share with you seven diva-licious recipes that are sure to make you a hit at your house, married or not. From there, I am sure you will find the courage to experiment on your own.

Diva Confession

I will purpose to make my home an oasis to all who enter. I will observe the rite of taking communion with my loved ones and friends by preparing and serving food for the body as well as the soul.

A Diva-licious Week of Recipes

Day One

Barbequed Chicken Wings
Coconut Rice
Tomato and Cucumber Slices

Barbequed Chicken Wings

Sauce:

6 Tablespoons soy sauce
1½ cups brown sugar
8 garlic cloves, (fresh or minced)
4 drops Tabasco sauce
1 cup BBQ sauce *(I like to combine
½ KC Masterpiece and ½ Sweet Baby Rays)*

¼ teaspoon dry mustard
½ cup water
4 chicken bouillon cubes
¼ cup white vinegar

Stir all of the above over medium heat for five minutes. Set aside.

Wings:

4-5 lbs. chicken wings
(Lightly salt and pepper, or use Lawry's Seasoned salt sparingly.)

Preheat oven to 450°. Place wings in a rectangular baking pan or roasting pan. Pour sauce over, cover and bake for 45 minutes to an hour. Take cover off for last 10 minutes to allow wings to brown.

Coconut Rice

2 cups rice
1 can Thai coconut milk
2 cups water
1 dash salt

Combine ingredients in a glass bowl. Cover, place in microwave, and cook for 20 minutes on High. If you have a microwave that is very powerful, cook 20 minutes on power level 5, then cook on High for additional 5 minutes if needed.

Tomato & Cucumber Slices

2 beefsteak tomatoes
2 cucumbers, peeled
¼ cup Italian dressing

Cut tomatoes and cucumbers into slices and garnish side of plate. Add a splash of Italian dressing.

Day Two

Quick 'n Easy Roast
Sautéed Cabbage

Quick 'n Easy Roast

1 3-lb. roast
Worcestershire sauce
1 can golden mushroom soup
4 medium potatoes, peeled
    and quartered

black pepper, thyme, and
    garlic powder
1 pkg dry onion soup mix
1 cup sliced carrots

Preheat oven to 325°. Line a roast pan with enough aluminum foil to form a tent.

Sprinkle roast with spices. Mix together soup, soup mix, and dash of Worcestershire. Pour over roast. Add potatoes and carrots around roast. Fold aluminum foil over to form a tented cover and bake for 2½ hours or until meat reaches desired doneness.

Sautéed Cabbage

4 slices turkey bacon
1 medium onion, diced
1½ teaspoons black pepper

1 head cabbage,
    shredded
1 Tablespoon sugar

Sauté turkey bacon in a large skillet until soft. Add cabbage and onion. Simmer on low until cooked and cabbage is soft. Sprinkle with sugar and pepper to taste.

Day Three

Homemade Vegetable Soup
Divine Chicken Salad
Italian Bread

Homemade Vegetable Soup

½ cup diced onion
3 cups sliced zucchini
1 cup chopped, seeded tomatoes
2 teaspoons fresh parsley, chopped
4 packets instant chicken broth
  and seasoning mix

4 garlic cloves, minced
1 cup sliced carrots
½ teaspoon basil
½ teaspoon pepper

In a nonstick Dutch oven, sauté onion, seasoning mix, and garlic. Cook until onion is translucent, about 5 minutes. Add remaining ingredients; cover and cook over low heat, stirring occasionally for approx. 10 minutes.

Add 4 cups water and bring to a boil. Reduce to medium heat, cover, and cook until vegetables are soft, about 20 minutes. Using a slotted spoon, remove about 1½ cup of the vegetables and set aside. In blender, purée remaining soup in two batches; return puréed mixture to saucepan. Add set-aside vegetables and heat. Serve with warm Italian bread.

Divine Chicken Salad

2 boneless, skinless chicken breasts
1 bunch seedless green grapes, halved
1 small package almond slivers
1 small onion (sweet or red), diced
lettuce leaves for garnish, if desired

¼ cup mayonnaise
1 teaspoon mustard
salt and pepper to taste
dash of sugar

Boil chicken breasts until cooked. Let cool and dice into
½-inch cubes. Combine in a large bowl with onion, grapes,
almonds, mayonnaise (add more if needed), and mustard.
Sprinkle with salt, pepper, and sugar to taste. Let sit in
refrigerator for an hour. Serve on top of lettuce leaves.

Day Four

Hot & Spicy Meatballs
Creamy Garlic Mashed Potatoes
Green Beans

Hot & Spicy Meatballs

Meatballs:

¾ lb. ground beef
¾ cup fine, dry bread crumbs
1½ Tablespoons minced onion
¾ teaspoon salt

½ teaspoon horseradish
3 drops Tabasco sauce
2 eggs, beaten
½ teaspoon pepper

Combine ingredients in a plastic bowl. Form into ¾-inch balls. Cook tenderly, turning until thoroughly cooked and brown; pour off drippings. Set aside.

Sauce:

¾ cup ketchup
1½ Tablespoons white vinegar
2 Tablespoons brown sugar
2 teaspoons Worcestershire sauce
¼ teaspoon pepper

½ cup water
1 Tablespoon minced onion
1 teaspoon dry mustard
3 drops Tabasco sauce
1½ teaspoons salt

Mix all ingredients together; pour over cooked meatballs. Cover and simmer 10 minutes. Stir occasionally.

Creamy Garlic Mashed Potatoes

3 medium potatoes, peeled and cubed
2 cloves garlic, roasted
2 Tablespoons heavy cream
1 Tablespoon extra virgin olive oil
1 teaspoon chopped parsley
salt and pepper to taste

In a large saucepan, add enough water to cover potatoes; add ½ teaspoon salt and bring to a rolling boil. Cook potatoes until soft when pierced, about 10 minutes. Drain all but 1-inch of water from the pot. Add garlic, cream, oil and parsley. Mash (or whip) potatoes until smooth, adding more cream if needed. Add salt and pepper to taste.

Green Beans

1 lb. fresh green beans, trimmed
¼ cup minced onion
½ teaspoon salt
¼ teaspoon garlic powder

Steam or sauté green beans with onion until tender. Sprinkle with salt and garlic powder.

Day Five

Spaghetti Casserole
Tossed Green Salad

Spaghetti Casserole

1 lb. ground beef
¼ cup chopped green pepper
1 can (10½ ounces) condensed
   cream of mushroom soup
1 soup can of water
1 cup shredded sharp
   process cheese

½ cup chopped onion
2 Tablespoons butter
1 can (10¾ ounces)
   condensed tomato soup
1 clove garlic, minced
½ lb. spaghetti, cooked
   and drained

Preheat oven to 350°. Sauté beef, onion, and pepper in butter until lightly browned and crumbly and vegetables are tender.

In a saucepan, combine soups, water, and garlic until heated through. Add ½ cup cheese and cooked spaghetti.

Combine spaghetti and ground beef in a 3-quart casserole dish. Top with remaining shredded cheese. Bake for 30 minutes. Serve with tossed salad.

Day Six

Roasted Salmon
Sautéed Spinach

Roasted Salmon

Sauce:

2 Tablespoons fresh lemon juice, warmed slightly
2 Tablespoons minced fresh ginger
2 Tablespoons snipped fresh chives
6 Tablespoons softened butter

Preheat oven to 500°. In a small bowl, blend juice, ginger, chives, and butter. Set aside at room temperature.

Salmon:

1 5 oz. salmon filet
salt and pepper to taste
4 Tablespoons olive oil

Sprinkle salmon lightly with salt and pepper. Cover bottom of oven-prove skillet with olive oil and heat. When oil is hot, add salmon, skin side-up and cook until nicely browned, about one minute. Turn fish over and put skillet in oven. Roast for about 4 minutes (for medium well). Test to make sure it's done by flaking with a fork. Top with butter sauce before serving.

Sautéed Spinach

2 Tablespoons olive oil
4 cups fresh spinach leaves, loosely packed
salt and pepper to taste
1 teaspoon minced garlic

Heat olive oil over medium-high in a large sauté pan. Add spinach, sprinkle with pepper, a dash of salt, and garlic. Sauté over medium heat until wilted. Serve with roasted salmon.

Day Seven

Yummy Chicken Sauté
Roasted Sweet Potatoes

Yummy Chicken Sauté

1 rotisseried chicken, deboned, sliced or shredded
1 cup red wine or cooking wine
1 cup chicken broth
2 cups frozen pearl onions
1 small carton of pre-sliced fresh mushrooms
1 package dry Good Seasons Italian dressing mix
2 Tablespoons minced fresh basil

Place chicken and remaining ingredients in a large skillet.
Simmer over medium-low heat for 25 minutes.

Roasted Sweet Potatoes

2 medium sweet potatoes, peeled and cut into ¼-inch thick
   slices
3 small red onions, peeled and cut into ½- to ⅜-inch thick slices
2 Tablespoons olive oil
½ teaspoon kosher salt
1½ teaspoons each roughly chopped fresh rosemary, thyme,
   and sage

Preheat oven to 450°. Combine vegetables, oil, salt, and herbs
in a bowl; toss to coat thoroughly. Arrange the vegetable slices
in a single layer without crowding on a large parchment or
foil-lined, rimmed baking sheet. Roast in oven for about 20
minutes until soft on the inside and browned on the edges.
Test with tip of a knife. Serve hot or at room temperature.

Diva-licious Garbage Salad
(Good as a meal in itself!)

1 small package fresh, pre-sliced mushrooms
1 small package shredded carrots
½ a large yellow pepper, diced
½ a large orange or red pepper, diced
½ a large cucumber, peeled and diced
1 tomato, diced, or a small carton of cherry tomatoes, halved
1 small can mandarin oranges
1 small package slivered almonds
dash of Lawry's Seasoned salt
½ small package crumbled blue cheese

Toss all ingredients with ¼ cup Wishbone Italian dressing.
Add more if desired.

3 Diva-licious Desserts

Banana Tortilla Crêpe
Maltby Cake
Banana Pudding

Banana Tortilla Crêpe

1 large flour tortilla
1 Tablespoon melted butter
1 teaspoon sugar
1 large box instant vanilla pudding
1 small container Cool Whip
1 Tablespoon vanilla extract
2 cups chopped bananas
½ cup slivered almonds
sprig of fresh mint

Preheat oven to 375°. Brush both sides of tortilla with melted butter and place in pie pan. Sprinkle with sugar. Bake until lightly brown, about 20 minutes. Cool completely. In a large bowl, combine pudding, Cool Whip, vanilla, and 1½ cups banana. Spread pudding mixture over half of tortilla. Fold in half. Top with remaining banana, almonds, and mint, if desired.

Maltby Cake

Cake:

1 box of white vanilla cake mix
1 small box instant chocolate pudding
1 small box instant vanilla pudding
½ cup oil

4 eggs
1 cup chocolate chips
1½ cups water

Preheat oven to 350°. In a large bowl, mix all of the above. Place in two 8-inch round cake pans. Bake for 30 minutes. Cool completely.

Frosting:

1 pint fresh whipping cream
1 Tablespoon instant vanilla pudding

Mix whipping cream with instant vanilla pudding and whip until thick. Frost cake. Place chocolate dipped strawberries around the top edge of cake and serve.

Banana Pudding

1 small box instant vanilla pudding
1 4-oz. package cream cheese
½ can Eagle Brand condensed milk
1 small container Cool Whip

1½ cups of milk
5 bananas, sliced
1 box of vanilla wafers

Mix pudding and milk. Beat until thick. Add cream cheese, condensed milk, and Cool Whip. Line the bottom of a 9 x 13 glass baking dish with wafers. Place a layer of sliced bananas on top of wafers. Spread a layer of pudding mixture on top. Continue to layer wafers, sliced bananas, and pudding until you reach the top of dish. Finish with final layer of pudding and refrigerate until firm. This pudding is also great as a dip for fresh fruit.

Now you have a wide variety of dishes with assorted flavors. You can feel free to pick and choose. According to your own preference, you can now hunt for other recipes that best fit your dietary needs, or simplify what has been offered here. For additional yummy recipes and more encouragement on developing this area of your life, I highly recommend reading two great books by dear friends of mine, *God Is in the Kitchen Too* by P.B. Wilson and *Life Giving* by Tammy Maltby. Remember, even in the kitchen one has to plan her work and work her plan. Also, log on to homemadegourmet.com for help with menu planning, recipes, cookbooks and even mixes you can buy to spice up a good meal!

In all aspects of life, a diva echoes the sentiments of the Proverbs 31 woman by always being prepared as much as she can be. Considering her future, she makes responsible choices to stand ready, dressed appropriately for the occasion, to address any person or circumstance in the right posture and impress the masses.

Her house is in divine order—her personal house and her spiritual house. Because she makes it a priority to take good care of herself and her household, she is able to balance her priorities and have a reserve to address the needs of those beyond her personal threshold. Her arms are extended outward because she understands that God has not blessed her with everything she has to make her a self-indulgent person. But rather the overflow and even some sacrifices must be made for those less fortunate than herself. Her hands reach out to the needy once the affairs of her own home are set in order and nothing is found lacking within her inner circle.

A diva, in true imitation of the divine nature of God, has a universal view of life. She seeks areas of need that she is qualified to fill and applies herself to those areas. She has a heart for those less fortunate than herself and her spirit is touched by their need. Whether taking the time to mentor young people, or spend time with the elderly who are ill or lonely, she leaves a lasting touch in the lives of those with needs that are ignored by many. She takes the time to make the overlooked feel special. Her touch is an extension of God's arms and a silent witness of His care and goodness.

Though she doesn't seek praise, she reaps it and her reputation precedes her within her sphere of influence—her home and her community. Her family is a testament of her care and attention. Her household speaks of the order she has established, as well as her eye for the details of all that transpires within its walls. Her husband reflects the grace and the love she showers on his life while walking on the firm foundation of her encouragement and prayers.

What separates this woman from all others? She does not rely solely on charm or beauty though they are clearly a part of her makeup. The foundation for her confidence is grounded in her relationship with her Lord and King. She has the heart of a worshipper. Her life is saturated with prayer, and she walks in complete surrender to God's instructions for her life. She has childlike faith that trusts God with every detail— the seasons, the timing, and the varying circumstances whether difficult or great. Her faith causes her to live consistently, radiating a calming force to all in her world. She keeps her eye on the big picture, choosing her battles wisely, and remains cognizant of what is truly important in the long run. She is not motivated by instant gratification but by lasting results. Therefore, she never judges by face value or the potential for great fruit by the size of the seed. She knows that a watermelon seed is smaller than that of a peach yet it bears greater fruit. She chooses the greater good among her choices for the sake of those she loves. Making her assessments carefully before speaking or moving.

She lives life generously. With her hands open, she seeks to give and give again, knowing that it is more blessed to give than receive. Her bounty is great, overflowing with generous portions of all that she gives. It is returned to her in greater measure because she walks in accordance with the law of sowing and reaping.

She lives life purposefully. Understanding the seasons and celebrating each one. She measures the time by applying herself to all her current season calls for. Nothing more, nothing less. She does not waste her emotions on discontent, but chooses joy deliberately, discerning that moments not treasured will later be remembered with regret for not embracing them fully. She lives in the present knowing it will be the past soon enough, while tomorrow cannot be predicted.

She lives life passionately. Using her natural giftings in harmony with her response to the needs around her stirs her heart. Small wonder she rises early and goes to bed late. She is consumed by enthusiasm! She enjoys her work and looks forward to it. Because she loves what she does, she is excellent and others are blessed by her contributions. Whether in the arena of business, charity, or personal, the joy for what she does is contagious to all she comes in contact with. Her love for what she does is translated into the finished product she presents.

She lives life delightfully, taking the time to smell the roses. To laugh, to feel, to dream, to love, and be loved. Though she is continually inspired by her profession, her profession does not consume her to the point where important relationships are damaged and the simple pleasures of life are overlooked. She seeks balance, taking on only the cares of today because she knows tomorrow will come with many more of its own. She focuses on the task at hand and leaves the rest to God and His timing. She lives in the present. Recording every laugh, every sigh in her memory. She doesn't allow a wandering mind to rob her of present pleasures and conversation. She truly hears what is being said to her because you have her undivided attention. Her focus produces not just genuine caring but clarity in understanding and discernment with all the details she is privy to.

She lives life creatively. Adding her own brand of wonderfulness to everything she touches. Her home, her wardrobe speak of her own brand of uniqueness. Her relationships are alive and vibrant because of what she imparts to others—kindness, faithfulness, and priceless wisdom. She causes others around her to delight in things they never noticed before. She treats each friendship as a precious gift that is never taken for granted. She shares unexpected gifts that reinforce a friend's value. For every problem there is a solution and she finds it. Creatively, unexpectedly, but always with good results.

She lives a centered life. Centered in the knowledge of her God, her purpose, and what is truly important. Because she is centered, she is sure-footed when the seasons of her life change. She adjusts without resistance or trepidation, valuing change as a necessary component of a life that explores and reaches its fullest potential. She takes one day at a time. Day by day. Season by season she comes into her own and allows others to do the same. Loving them as they are and caring about them too much to allow them to settle for sameness or mediocrity.

Perhaps the greatest part of the divine nature we share with God as blessed divas is the power to effect change in the lives of others. Ooh...the stories I could tell about more divine divas, but the bottom line is simply this: Whether close loved ones or more neutral associates, the touch of a true diva will always be felt beneath the skin. Deep in the heart of the inner man or woman. A word spoken, a deed done, a silent gesture that resounds in the minds and hearts of all she encounters. The effect is the same. Changed minds, changed lives, and a moment of wonder, "How divine was she!"

Diva Confession

I will live not to make my own personal statement, but to reflect the power and compassion of God. I will be an open vessel of His creativity, influence, and passion for mankind. I will be an imitator of His divine nature and a lasting blessing to all around me.

Diva Do's and Don'ts

๏ Celebrate your unique qualities as a woman and work them to the max!

- Confess that you are not superwoman and that's all right.

- Do what you can and leave the rest to God.

- Get help when you need it.

- Plan your work and work your plan.

- Set priorities and realistic boundaries for your time and affairs.

- Do not overlook relationships in lieu of productivity. Make time for both in your schedule.

- Take an honest assessment of your giftings and passions and choose your work within those guidelines.

- Always seek to bless before being blessed.

- Do not help others into paralysis, partner with them to live up to their full potential.

- Get your finances in order.

- Prepare for the future and set realistic goals for yourself and your family.

- Seek to hear before being heard; that way you won't miss a thing.

- Set your house in order. Make it a comfortable home.

- Take time to delight in the little things.

- Live in the moment and treasure it.

- Rest in the promises of God for your life and trust Him with the various seasons that are sure to confront you.

Div-otion

Grace and peace be yours in abundance through the knowledge of God and of Jesus our Lord. His divine power has given us everything we need for life and godliness through our knowledge of him who called us by his own glory and goodness. Through these he has given us his very great and precious promises, so that through them you may participate in the divine nature and escape the corruption in the world caused by evil desires. For this very reason, make every effort to add to your faith goodness; and to goodness, knowledge; and to knowledge, self-control; and to self-control, perseverance; and to perseverance, godliness; and to godliness, brotherly kindness; and to brotherly kindness, love. For if you possess these qualities in increasing measure, they will keep you from being ineffective and unproductive in your knowledge of our Lord Jesus Christ (2 Peter 1:2-8).

Dear heavenly Father, I am so happy that I am Your child. Teach me Your ways and instill Your virtues in me that I might be a true reflection of Your divine nature. Help me to live each day in such a way that the lives of others are the better for it. Let my testimony be one of victory, peace, and everlasting joy. In the name of the One who reigns forever in my heart, Jesus. Amen.

Recommended Reading

Thrive: A Woman's Guide to a Healthy Lifestyle
by Carrie Carter, M.D.
Only a Woman by Terri McFaddin
Becoming a Woman of Beauty & Strength
by Elizabeth George
A Wise Woman Once Said by Shirley Rose
Intimate Issues by Lorraine Pintus and Linda Dillow
The Urban Guide to Biblical Money Management
by Oteia Bruce
The Total Money Makeover and Financial Peace
by Dave Ramsey
Fit for Life by Harvey Diamond
The Answer Is in Your Blood Type
by Joseph Christiano and Steven Weissberg

Other Books by Michelle McKinney Hammond

What to Do Until Love Finds You
Secrets of an Irresistible Woman
The Power of Femininity
Get a Love Life
If Men Are Like Buses Then How Do I Catch One?
What Becomes of the Brokenhearted
How to Be Blessed and Highly Favored
Get Over It and On With It
Why Do I Say "Yes" When I Need to Say "No?"
Sassy, Single, & Satisfied
The Unspoken Rules of Love

To correspond with Michelle McKinney Hammond,
you may write to her:
c/o HeartWing Ministries
P.O. Box 11052
Chicago, IL 60611
E-mail her at heartwingmin@yahoo.com
Or log on to her website at:
www.michellehammond.com or www.heartwing.org
For information on booking her for a speaking engagement
Contact Speak Up Speaker Services at
1-810-982-0898